Dear Linda,

What a [...]
the workshops. You [...]
[...] a breath
Keep listening:
others
It is one
highest

[...] your ear!
to God,
yourself.
of life's
callings...
Steve
5/10/97

MW01355511

LISTEN
TO YOUR

NEIGHBOR'S
HEART

STEVE POWERS

The Listener's Press

A book about the Awesome POWER of Listening

LISTEN
TO YOUR

NEIGHBOR'S
HEART

"Our lives are filled with greater peace and purpose as we seek to hear the voice within and compassionately listen to a world calling to be heard"

STEVE POWERS

LISTEN TO YOUR NEIGHBOR'S HEART
Copyright © 1997 by Steve Powers

Cover design by David Wink
(614)-387-8267

All rights reserved
Printed in the United States of America

No part of this book may be used or reproduced
in any manner whatsoever without written
permission except in the case of brief
quotations embodied in critical
articles and reviews.

For information contact:

The Listener's Press
356 North Townview Circle
Mansfield, Ohio 44907
(419)-756-9117

ISBN 0-9654075-0-0

Library of Congress
Catalog Card Number: 96-94690

Acknowledgements
A big *THANK YOU* to...

...My kids Jeremy, Elizabeth, and Mikey who have provided me with frequent opportunities to sharpen my listening skills. Perhaps more importantly have been the times they have amazed me with their ability to listen to friends and family members with a degree of sensitivity and empathy usually reserved for adults. They have been three of my best teachers.

...My wife Sue, who although daily surrounded (bombarded) at school by students and colleagues wanting to be heard and at home with her own kids and friends in need of an ear, still makes the time and finds the energy to listen to her husband's concerns, complaints, and sometimes silly notions. I am most appreciative that she continued to encourage me to finish this book (when often I had no desire to!) and regularly asked, "How's it going?"

...My dad, who by his actions taught me what it meant to reach out to our neighbors' hearts. He spent many a long evening in the troubled city of Camden, New Jersey, helping to remodel a store into a youth and community center, playing pickup basketball with a group of kids, and befriending young boys who did not know or have a relationship with their fathers. Simply being there and listening was his ministry.

...My many graduate students who faithfully read varying forms of the book, diplomatically giving me suggestions and feedback along the way. Four individuals in particular need special recognition—Kathleen Higgins, Candice Johnson, Nancy Starn, and Vicki Dye. They really took to heart my challenge to review, critique, and in general, pick the book apart—diligently correcting grammar, making word changes, proofreading, adding creative touches, and lending words of encouragement.

Kathleen even recruited a gifted colleague, Peggy Nesbit, to join in the editing fun. Her exquisite writing ability, wonderful suggestions, and twelfth hour labors were a God-send. Peggy's expertise provided just what this manuscript needed to refine it into a book worthy of reading. Plus, I made a new friend!

...My typist extraordinaire, Shirl Johnson. She marvelously took my handwritten scrawls (arrows, inserts, spelling mistakes, and all) and translated them into something readable on the computer. This is when the book really began to take shape and become a reality for me.

...My computer whiz, promotional genius, and all-around good guy brother-in-law, Tedd Long. His computer technical support (he saved my computer from many sledge hammer bludgeonings!), business sense, and marketing ideas were invaluable.

...My graphic artist, David Wink. His vision and creative touches on the cover captured the spirit of the book's message.

...My last minute heros, Mike Ruhe and Kathy Frye. They helped put the finishing touches on David's wonderful artwork.

My erstwhile friend, Renée Gisclon, who I think if the truth be told, did not really know what she was getting herself into by saying "yes" to the request to be my editor. I recall telling her that the manuscript was fairly refined and most likely only needed a few changes here and there. I'm sure I probably did a lousy job at attempting to hide my shock when she returned the first edited portion. There must have been at least 10—12 little red marks on every page! I guess I wasn't quite done after all!

Renée and Peggy were particularly adept at standing their ground in the face of my repeated attempts to change their minds about keeping something in that actually needed to be tossed out. Writers become far too married to their words. Skilled and compassionate editors can help make the separation less painful.

...My good friends and colleagues—some who have entered my life for a five minute encounter, others who have graced it for a lifetime. Their times of understanding, support, and challenge continue to leave their indelible mark. To name all of you would take an entire chapter. Plus I fear I would leave one of you out.

I know who you are, *and* so do you. *Thanks*...

Dedication

The following is the eulogy I gave at my mother's memorial service and is a tribute to the influence she had on my life and my writing. It was the toughest talk I have ever had to give. This book is for you, Mom!

Parents and their kids have an important relationship with one another. Perhaps because of its uniqueness, there seems to be a very special connection between fathers and daughters, mothers and sons. And so it was with my mom—that little wink, nod, and smile—that special understanding.

She never got a college degree, but taught me more about life than the best professor I ever had. She never received any special training in how to help people but helped more people than most social workers I know. She knew she could never make things all better when I hurt, but she gave me what I needed by her listening ears, open mind, caring heart, and extra measure of unconditional love—the kind which communicated "I understand and accept where you are and how you feel—no matter what."

She allowed me to fail because sometimes life's lessons come the hard way. Most of all she simply let me be me—never trying to make me be who she wanted me to be or to change me. Rather, she sought to nurture and guide me.

My mom may have been diminutive in stature, quiet with her thoughts, and at times just seem to blend into a room without even noticing her, but she had great reserves of inner strength, self- awareness, concern for others, and wisdom.

I remember how slow she was to anger: but when she felt an injustice had been done or that something was unfair, how quick and sure of herself she was in responding. I recall a funny moment, when in a state of exasperation at a reckless driver, she looked at me and huffed, "I wish I had a big truck right now!"

I think back upon the many school projects she helped me with, the outrageous Halloween costumes we conjured up, and

3

the terrific days we spent at the Jersey shore.

I vividly recollect my first few months of college—more than 700 miles away from home. My mom typed a few of my papers in New Jersey and sent them out to me at Taylor University in Indiana. Or how about the time I came home after my first three weeks away, lugging every ounce of clothing I owned—unwashed of course! No one could quite iron a shirt like my mom.

I'll always remember what a great baseball player she thought I was. Some of my fondest memories are the times in high school when I would look up from my position at first base—home and away games—only to see our most loyal and often solitary fan—my mom. No wonder I thought I might make it to the big leagues one day. She was my biggest fan—on and off the field.

She was my champion. How proud she was too when I graduated from graduate school knowing that she had taken a part-time job to help put me through.

Mom was often our family's emotional thermostat, helping to adjust and bring balance to the moods of the sometimes three rather moody family members with whom she lived!

She taught me the value of a word of encouragement, note of thanks, and look of understanding.

She demonstrated the art of kindness by how she lived her life.

What a sight it was to see this little woman driving a big old yellow church bus—stick shift, pillows piled high on top of the seat, no power steering and all—as she maneuvered around town picking up anxious kids for their trip to weekly Bible school.

Christmas was always a special time in my life—especially when I found the "perfect" gift for my mom—copper jello molds. I rushed home, delighted with my purchase, and went about wrapping them. I could hardly wait for Christmas morning. I watched with anticipation as she opened her present. It came later in the morning because she always looked on with such delight as the rest of us opened ours.

As she pulled out her gifts and held them up, she had a smile on her face as if she had just received a diamond necklace. And you know something, I think to her there wasn't any difference.

What a wonderful grandmom she was to Jeremy and little Elizabeth. She spent countless hours reading to Jeremy (as she did with me), playing games, and making his favorite breakfast— oatmeal. He wouldn't eat it anyplace else but at Grandmom's.

When Elizabeth was six weeks old, Mom and Dad came to Ohio to visit and it was my mom who really got her to begin chattering and "talking." She would sit with, talk, and sing to Elizabeth for hours. She indeed possessed the patience of Job. If you ever witnessed her perseverance in solving a crossword or jigsaw puzzle you would quickly agree. I only wish I had caught more of that from her!

Many years ago, when I was more broke than usual, my mom had given me a few bucks before heading back to Ohio. Since my college days, it had always been Dad's custom to tuck a twenty dollar bill in my hand as I was about to depart for the Midwest. As I was saying goodbye and about to board the plane, Dad handed me his welcomed gift of $20. I began to tell him that Mom had already given me some money when I saw my mom in the background waving her hands, shaking her head, and mouthing the words, "Don't say anything. Just take it!"

It was my mom, who during a very difficult and painful time in my life, helped me to see things in a completely new light. As she was listening to me describe how discouraged I was feeling about things, she patiently waited for me to finish, and then she spoke these most powerful words. "You know, Steve, if you could live with any family for more than a few days, you would discover that no one lives a 'normal' life."

All of a sudden, what I was feeling and experiencing took on a new perspective. She was helping me in a way to say, "Don't be so hard on yourself, Steve. You are human and we all make mistakes. But that doesn't make you any less of a person. Let go and be kind to yourself. It isn't all your fault, and when the smoke

5

clears, things will get better." In her gentle way she once again taught me that, yes, just like a bad call in a game, life is not always fair. It's normal to feel hurt, anger, and remorse, but we can and must work through it.

My mom did not quite understand many of what she would call today's "new women" who seemingly spend much of their lives trying to, in the vernacular, "find themselves."

She discovered who she was in the relationships with her family, her friends, and her God.

She derived meaning and purpose in her work, her leisure, and her loved ones.

Balance, simplicity, and one day at a time were her watchwords. Her sense of humor, ability to laugh at herself as well as the the little things in life, compassion for and interest in others, and faith in God were not lost on me. She passed them on to everyone she touched and helped to make each individual feel important and like a person of worth.

In a word, my mom was "*affirming.*"

My mom was my greatest encourager as a writer. Years ago she typed the first draft of this book and, when I found out it was in the improper form, she typed it again! I think what she enjoyed the most about my writing was the chance to get to know her son better. I was never the most open person. Without the groundwork she laid, this book would have never become a reality.

My mom would not have been very comfortable with hearing all of these platitudes in person because of how humble and unassuming she was. Well, Mom, now they can be said for everyone to hear. Besides, those of us who knew you already realized this stuff about you.

Our lives will never be the same with your absence but we are richer for it because of your presence. And you will be with us in memory and what you brought to each of our lives. You have given us much more than we could ever give back to you.

We take heart in the fact that you knew where you were going after this short time on earth, and that we one day would join you in eternity. These words from I Corinthians ring true in our heart, spirit, and soul. They are our refuge. They bring us comfort. We love and miss you, Mom.

"Death has been swallowed up in victory.
Where O death is your victory? Where O death is your sting?"

Mom, if patience is indeed a virtue, then you are now wearing a glorious crown.

If love is really the greatest gift of all, then the space under your Christmas tree is overflowing, Mom.

And, Mom, if the meek truly do inherit the earth, then the whole wide world is in your hands.

Mom, this time it's you that hit the home run and I'm watching you from the stands—admiring, rooting, and cheering you on.

And, oh yeah, Mom...

I brushed my teeth real well last night.

I'm using a lot more sunscreen these days.

And I almost made us late this morning! (I guess some things never change, eh?)

Thanks for *everything,* Mom.

(As I type this eulogy and read it for the first time in several years, it strikes me that when a compassionate listener dies, the whole world mourns her loss.)

Introduction
(Don't Skip This!)

It was halfway through the evening Christmas program that my mind began to wander as my eyes surveyed the congregation. "What's going on with her?" I thought while noticing my friend Mary in the pew ahead of me, head bowed, and trembling ever so slightly. A tissue wiped away a tear as she quietly left the service and exited through the side door.

I would like to say that I immediately sensed her need to talk with someone. But if the truth be told, I had lost interest in the sermon and looked upon Mary's departure and possible desire to have someone follow her as my opportunity to leave before I fell asleep. The service was fine and uplifting for most. Lack of interest was more my problem.

I found Mary in the church office already talking to another friend. Since I was in my second year of graduate school in counseling, I felt perhaps I could be of further assistance. I was not prepared for what took place. In retrospect, I now realize that this encounter was to have greater impact on my understanding of the listening and helping process than any class or training I had ever taken.

For twenty minutes, Mary proceeded to alternately cry, express her feelings, and sit in silence. The sound of the organ reverberating and the congregation singing signaled the end of the service. Standing up while drying her eyes, Mary tugged at her dress, gave a half smile and hug, thanked us, and left.

"Well, Powers, you really did it this time. A few months away from completing your degree in counseling and you didn't even know what her problem was! You never even asked her what was troubling her. Great work. Big help you were..."

This verbal and mental assault continued through the following week as I further questioned my skills and competence. When Friday arrived, I received a little note in the mail from—of all

8

people—Mary. Before reading it, the feelings of inadequacy and guilt over my perceived mishandling of the situation surfaced in full force.

With a bit of trepidation similar to opening one's report card, I began to read the following handwritten lines:

"Dear Steve, Thank you for your time and caring the other night. It helped me so much in knowing what to do.

"Love, Mary."

I sat in stunned silence, not realizing the full impact of what Mary's note would come to mean to me. I was just beginning to understand the mighty power of the listening ear. I could begin to hear the admonitions of my counseling supervisors echoing in my mind as they said, "Counseling is listening, and listening is counseling. We truly help others by helping them to *hear themselves*. We must listen more closely to the *feelings* which many times lie just beneath the facts they are describing. We often become far too caught up in the details of their story. Don't talk *to* them or *at* them. Remain interested, attentive, and *LISTEN*."

Would it surprise you to know that to this day I still am not aware of what the problem was in Mary's life? All I know is that Mary received both some relief and direction that Sunday evening because two people who were attempting to care about and listen to her *feelings* allowed her to express and explore a troubling aspect of her life. Once out on the table, she then—*on her own*— began to see some things from a new perspective, get more in touch with her pain, and set into motion the steps necessary to deal with the situation.

It has been just this type of experience along with many listening encounters, as both the speaker and listener, that has encouraged me to share some of my thoughts on the topic with you. As I survey the spectrum of human relationships and seemingly infinite variety of struggles with which we all must deal, I have never been *more convinced* that every human being has a tremendous need to be loved *and* listened to.

My need was never any greater than while in graduate school; and it was through the caring, thoughtful, and often selfless ears of some very good friends that I began to discover parts of myself that I never knew or was unwilling and unable to admit existed. They helped me to unlock feelings, needs, ideas, and dreams that were waiting to be opened. In turn this gave me the strength and increased wisdom to continue on this path to greater self-awareness, understanding, and acceptance.

Encouraged to be more open, I felt a new and exciting *transformation* begin to take place within. Hearing myself helped me to not only be more at peace with who I was but also enlarged my vision of both wanting and knowing how to hear what others and God were saying. Listening had dynamic ramifications on all aspects of my life. It added a new and rich dimension to my world.

What I have attempted to do in this little book is relate a few of the ideas I have discussed in the classroom with social work students; taught in workshops; presented to civic, church, and professional groups; and gleaned from the hundreds of hours spent listening to people whose problems spanned the range of low self-esteem to alcoholism. Perhaps, most importantly, it is what I have learned from the countless times I was listened to.

The world surely does not need another self-help book and the very least of my intentions is to provide one more to the endless inventory at the local bookstore. What has moved me more than anything towards penning these words has been the dearth of any books even remotely related to the art of listening. They just aren't out there.

My career has been spent either conducting or attending workshops on personal growth, on how to help students, on ways to assist people who hurt, and on developing skills to better connect with others. I have read, researched, and heard just about every guru or expert expounding upon the latest and best theory or formula for living. Each pays homage to the importance of listening, yet very few spend any serious time covering it.

This book was not written with the usual format of chapters or "how to" lists but with a combination of suggestions, questions, thoughts, feelings, reflections, anecdotes, and challenges for you to peruse at your leisure. Read them one at a time or all at once, starting at page one or beginning at the end.

This is less of a "how to" book
and more of an encouraging "*go do*" one.

Note: If you are studying this topic in a group or as a class, may I suggest that you each read a few pages and comment about the ideas that particularly spoke to you. Between sessions mark any passages that caught your attention or hit home. Discuss them at the next meeting. Complete the little "homework" assignments and try some of the suggestions sprinkled throughout. When you get back together report on how you did.

Chat about what you read with your kids, students, colleagues, friends, partners, and loved ones. Share your hopes, desires, and struggles in wanting to become a better listener. Talk about how you can incorporate the skill of listening into your lives more. Ask people you trust, and whose honesty you can handle, to give you feedback. Find mentors who are terrific listeners and allow them to nurture you in this area.

My desire for you is the same one I hold for every audience to which I speak, student I teach, and friend I encounter. If you need a push to become a better listener, I trust you will find a nudge from something here. If you need more of a shove, I hope that you might be struck more directly. And if you are already well on your way to becoming a skilled listener, my intent is that you will be affirmed for your efforts. We all need to hear "You're on the right track," "Keep up the good work," and "Nice job."

I can ask no more than that you reflect upon the thoughts in this book, seek to heighten your awareness to a world around you that calls to be heard, and consider how you may become more of a listener to the many people in your life.

It is well worth the effort, my friend...

Author's Note
(Don't Skip This Either!)

It's hard to believe that I wrote much of this book during a one-week period in the summer of 1983. Now, almost thirteen years later, I find myself cleaning it up a bit, changing a few words, and adding some new thoughts.

So, what happened during this time you are wondering?

Do you have a few days to listen? In a nutshell, I got caught up (more like swept away!) in that condition with which we all struggle—"terminal humanness."

If you are anything like me (and my hunch is that you are), your life is also about 180° from the consistency of the ocean's predictable tides. Rather, it is filled with change—some you asked for and some you did not. It is ripe with emotion—from unrelenting pain to unbridled joy. It has long periods of routine, interrupted by times of crisis and people just being people. One day feels peaceful within while the next may revolve around chaos. Each new day is an adventure at best.

If none of these words and thoughts seem to make sense or strike a chord whatsoever, you should be reading a different book. And don't ask me what because I don't think it's been written yet!

Much of this book was written during a time of both great pain and great hope. Some things in my life were coming to a screeching halt while other areas held much promise. Housing two such seemingly opposite feelings provided an amazingly rich source of energy. The gains were still a faint glimmer down the highway while the losses seemed ready to devour me.

During the next few years of my life, change and its myriad banquet of feelings became my constant companion. Unfortunately, or as I am beginning to say more often—fortunately—so was much of the resultant pain. All change—big and small, good or bad—involves some pain and discomfort. And our lives will never quite be the same. They can't.

Life can actually become much better. But it often comes only after the smoke clears as we sort out some of the pain and learn from the lessons. And so it has been in my life. The past fourteen years has found me burying a much too young and wonderful mom and grandmom, saying goodbye to my precious son, ending some once very important and comfortable relationships, leaving a fulfilling job, experiencing a few house fires, doing continual battle with a bout of malignant melanoma, and learning a little more about the meaning of the word *unfair*.

This time also brought into my life new and meaningful friendships, people who cared, two more beautiful children, a challenging career, a renewed sense of purpose and peace, and a greater desire to live more in the present and less in the past or future.

Oh yes, I also decided I should be spending a lot more time with the best listener in my life—so I married her!

While I would not trade any of the pain or joy I've experienced since I wrote part one of this book, life's lessons do indeed frequently come the hard way. They exact a price. It is in the difficulties, struggles, and on some of the seemingly darkest days that we encounter the brightest light and deepest meaning of our existence. Often it is during these periods of pain, discouragement, and wondering where God is in all of this that we discover *purpose*. It is truly the tough times and hurt that will define who we are now and, in turn, who we will become.

Passed on to me were the following words...

"It's not the wound that determines the quality of life, it's what you do with the wound—how you hold it, carry it, dance with it or bury yourself under it. Life is what happens as you live with the wounds. Life is not a matter of getting the wounds out of the way so you can finally live."

Martin Buber said that *"all suffering prepares the soul for vision."* And so often it is in this glorious gift of *sight* that we truly begin to hear the heart of another.

When issues surface and our pain rises up, we are compelled to listen to what is speaking to us. If we refuse or are unable to heed our feelings, the pain does not go away but comes out sideways in all of our life's relationships. It continues to affect and infect our well-being and quality of life. In working on and out our own *stuff*, we become better able to hear the *stuff* of others.

What has struck me so vividly these past several years is asking the question, "What do I really have to lose by being more open and honest with my thoughts, fears, hopes, pain, and feelings? Some friends perhaps? Or a bit of conditional love and acceptance from a few others? Or how about a diminished sense of self esteem and 'O.K-ness?'"

The great paradox is simply that *weakness* is actually *strength*.

For it takes more courage and strength to tell someone who we are and what is going on inside of us than to pretend we never hurt or to hide behind the guise of being strong.

Being open to our feelings, going through and coming out the other side with them, gives us *new eyes, ears, and hearts of compassion*. And when it is all said and done, what greater meaning can we derive from life than to genuinely connect with another—to hear and to be heard—to be there for a fellow human being as others have been there for us?

The memories we create with our children and loved ones by the magic of our listening ears and through our heart's connection is the true enduring legacy we leave them.

This has been my story through the many changes and passages. And I suspect it may be a bit of yours too. I am filled with gratitude for the people who have joined me on the journey. I am indebted to those who heard without wanting to fix everything and listened without judgment. I have appreciated the friends who took the time and risk to read between the lines or pick up on the things I could not, or perhaps would not, say. They helped give the unspoken within me a voice.

Especially courageous have been the listeners who did not

14

always take at face value everything I said. When not convinced by an answer or platitude I might give to the question of "how are you doing Steve?" they would be quick to respond with a gentle nudge of "No, Steve, how are you *really* doing?" I don't know where I'd be without them.

They brought comfort to me in the midst of deaths and separations too painful to ignore. They gave me hope after a diagnosis of cancer, surgery, and treatments. They showed me love after a near fatal house fire and faith through life changes much too difficult to face alone.

Listening becomes a kind of lifeline to our world that connects us to others, God, and ourselves. As the lighthouse illuminates a ship's path through the dark and stormy seas, a true listener shines like a beacon of light, hope, and direction in our lives.

Skilled Listeners know when to push and when to back off. When to go for it and when to let up. When to challenge us and when to just be there. For people at ease and at home with themselves, it comes pretty naturally.

Genuine Listeners have a sense of *mindfulness* about them— working on becoming their best self, decorating their own soul, and feeding their own spirit—for their feelings flow out to every person they touch.

Healthy Listeners draw from the wellspring of their abundance, giving from their reservoir of positive feelings and the personal growth work they have done in their own life.

Compassionate Listeners relate from their personal times of pain and difficult experiences. They have the ability to pass on their rich life's lessons while at the same time hearing the unique tones and nuances of ours. Sincerity and empathy are their constant companions.

Good Listeners are too few and far between. Hold them in the highest regard for they are a rare treasure.

Treat them as golden...
...and be thankful.

The Powers Listening and Compassion Quotient (PLaCQ)

Try this little quiz before you begin the book. It will serve to help you discover a few of your strengths and weaknesses when it comes to your ability to listen with empathy, understanding, and clarity. Please respond with one of the following answers:

1 = Never 2 = Sometimes 3 = Frequently 4 = Always

1.____ I am good at keeping what a speaker tells me confidential.

2.____ I am fairly open with my own thoughts and feelings.

3.____ I am able routinely to express warmth, caring, and respect.

4.____ I tend not to want to fix the problem(s) someone is having. My general philosophy is that a person with a problem or concern should do most of the work in discovering some of the answers.

5.____ I work at and take seriously being an honest, sincere, and genuine person.

6.____ I know the difference between sympathy and empathy and am able to communicate in primarily an empathic, rather than sympathetic, manner.

7.____ I am okay with the fact that some people may not feel much better and in fact could possibly feel worse after talking to me about what's on their minds or hearts.

8.____ I listen more for the feelings a speaker may be expressing than I do to the facts or details of their story.

9.____ I am aware of my own feelings and reactions as I listen to the feelings and concerns of another.

10.____ I am good at feeling as if I were the speaker (getting into their shoes); however, at the same time I can separate myself from him and not take on his issues or problems.

11.____ I do not feel like a failure as a helper or listener when the speaker does not take my suggestions, get better right away, or make any positive changes.

12.____ I am able to listen without being preoccupied by what to say next or by thinking up the perfect response for the speaker.

13.____ I am aware when I have a particular attitude, bias, or prejudice towards a certain speaker or his situation, work hard to manage it, and then continue to try to listen effectively.

14.____ I make a lot of non-verbal gestures such as nodding, smiling, grimacing, and other hand/body/facial movements, etc. when listening to another.

15.____ I am comfortable with silence in a listening encounter.

16.____ I think (and some people even tell me) that I have a good sense of humor.

17.____ I listen more with my eyes than I do my ears.

18.____ I am at ease with my own and other's tears.

19.____ While growing up I had at least one adult who really listened to me and/or who modeled healthy and effective listening.

20.____ I am not easily distracted, and if I do get off the the track, am quick to return to what the speaker is saying.

21.____ I value and maintain good eye contact.

22.____ I often make the effort to pause and check out and/or clarify what the speaker is saying in order to insure that I am hearing him correctly and what he is truly trying to tell me.

23.____ I place a high priority upon my own well-being, personal growth, and self-care.

24.____ I have one or more terrific listeners in my life who I can talk to on a regular basis—about just about anything!

25.____ I feel and know I am a good listener.

Add up the answers and put your score here _____

0-25 = Hello... Are you breathing? Call 911 quick!

26-40 = You need more help than I can give you! What's up?

41-55 = You've got a good start. Now keep going...

56-70 = You are doing some fine listening. What do you need to do to move into the elite class? Check all of your #1 & #2 answers.

71-85 = Well done. There must be a lot of people who appreciate you (or should appreciate you!) for being such a good listener.

86-100 = Put out your shingle and open up a private practice! You can probably skip reading this book too!! Ask for a refund!!!

If you scored under 86 then keep reading!

Did I Hear That Phone Message Right?

It was late—really late—and I was road weary. We had just made the long trip back from a wonderful week in Vermont—a place where time seems to stand still. My two traveling companions were all but out on their feet, and definitely out for the night. I was in my usual post-trip mode—wired! It was back to reality, and that included skimming a week's worth of newspapers, reading the mail, and an almost compulsory check of the answering machine.

That one-eyed blinking monster beckons me in much the same manner my post office box did while away at college. How did we ever manage to live without these things and, for that matter, such modern marvels as call waiting and fast food restaurants? Give me a break...

The light was flashing feverishly. I counted at least thirteen consecutive blinks which indicated thirteen people had called. I guessed several hang-ups, a salesperson or two announcing my free dance lessons, and a couple of friends. I sat slouched on the sofa dutifully listening to each message. It's the least I could do in honor of all those folks who courageously talked to my machine. (I hate them too.)

"Hi, Steve," "Hello, Mr. Powers," and beep, beep, beep went several of the hang-ups until I came to the following:

"Powers! Hey, Powers!! Yo, Powers!!! Are you there? I know you're there. Pick it up...!" (brief pause)

"Hi, Steve. It's your old buddy Susan here. I'm sorry you aren't home right now because I had a lot I needed to talk about. But what the heck, I'm going to talk to you anyway! Yesterday I..."

And so it went for about the next twenty minutes—Susan expressing thoughts and feelings about her job, family, finances, and just about anything else under the sun. She concluded with, "You know, Steve, I really do wish you were here to talk to but I feel a lot better just talking to your machine! Give me a call when you get a chance, OK?"

I managed a chuckle and shake of my head, wondered out loud if I had really heard what I thought I had heard, unpacked a few things, and went to bed. The next morning my wife Sue asked if there were any important messages or pieces of mail to discuss.

Since I was still in a bit of a funk from a full day of traveling and then only getting about four hours of sleep that night I said, "Well I think there was this one call from Susan, but it was so different that I'm not actually sure if I was dreaming it. Let me go check the machine."

That day I ran a number of errands and generally worked on getting back to life as usual. But I couldn't get that interesting phone message off my mind. The longer I thought about her call, the more it spoke to me. People need to be listened to, Steve. Remember your mentors and professors continually bombarding you in school with that thought as you were learning to be a counselor?

"Listen. Listen. Then listen some more," they would admonish. "The greatest help you can be to the one speaking is to give them your ears and your fullest attention." And even though Susan did not get a live listener on the other end of the line, the opportunity she seized to get some concerns off her shoulders and out of her heart gave her a good start on seeing them a little differently.

There are phone answering machines that are passive, allow the speaker to talk uninterrupted, and give no responses.

There are human answering machines which seek to control the conversation as well as manage and fix the speaker.

And then there are human listening machines which desire to truly hear, interact, challenge, and support.

There's a world of difference!

Which one are you?

*****

Now on to the book!

The longest and most difficult journey that many of us will ever embark upon is the twelve short inches it takes to get from our head to our heart. We may understand and think about things, but it can be so hard for us to feel and experience them.

Knowing and *doing* are often continents apart.

*****

Listening is a universal language which says to another,
"I value and care about you."
It serves to pay them one of life's highest compliments.

*****

The giving of our ears to another is one of life's ultimate gifts. Want to give a unique and thoughtful Christmas, valentine, or birthday gift this year? Look no further than your ears. Give that special person a handwritten note expressing your desire to make more of an effort throughout the year to genuinely be a better listener for him or her. Now that's a commitment!

*****

To listen is to *Risk*.

We risk not only hearing something that we are unwilling or incapable of taking in but also risk having to contend with those uncomfortable feelings and issues that strike a chord inside us. As we hear what is on another's mind and heart, similar experiences cannot help but surface within us. Relating to their pain resurrects our own. One person's struggle with relationships, personal and family problems, or sense of worth taps into our own. How can this not help but happen? We're human.

If you find yourself listening more to the feelings and experiences *within yourself* than to the person who triggered them, it could be a strong message that you need to seek a listener who will help in your own sorting-out process.

*****

Good listeners are willing to work on their own stuff and are usually able to tuck away or quiet the rumblings within themselves long enough to really hear what another is saying. If

20

this does not happen, the listener may harmfully begin to transfer or project his own issues on to the speaker. This can be a real mistake because the listener may miss the different tones and nuances unique to the speaker's pain and circumstance.

Remember, what might be true for you in your experience as the listener may very well not be true for the speaker's situation.

*****

To listen genuinely to another is also to *risk* getting involved, and I'm just not sure I want to be involved with you at this time.

It could be I'm too busy or preoccupied, uninterested, tired, or unable to hear you right now. Or maybe it's just too *RISKY!*

*****

The other big *risk* of listening? The "Big C"—CONTROL!

You got it, gang? Or should I say, "you really don't have it folks." For isn't much of what we like to think is control only an illusion? And those of us who admit to leaning a bit on the controlling side (let's see those hands!) tend to want to be in charge of a conversation.

The best and most effective listeners I know are okay when the ball is in the other person's court. They go with the flow for their sense of control or the *risk* of losing control isn't an issue.

*****

*Listening to others may perhaps help them to
truly hear themselves for the first time in their life. What a gift!*

*****

We Listen...
...*Well* with our *ears,*
...*Better* with our *eyes,*
...*Best* with our *HEARTS.*

*****

For many, feelings are like a far away country—a place that has never been visited or experienced. To help another get closer to his feelings and self is to help him discover a new and exciting piece of his world and life.

Listening to your heart,
finding out who you are
is not simple.
It takes time for the chatter to
quiet down.
In the silence of "not doing"
we begin to know what we
feel.
If we listen and hear what is
being offered, then anything
in life can be our guide.
Listen...

Author Unknown

*****

It is in listening to and understanding another that we
gain a sense of who he is and what he values as a human being.
Be warned, however, because this very encounter may demand
that we take stock of ourselves and what we value in our own life!

*****

The energy we give to another through our listening and
understanding is often converted by the speaker into greater
insight, courage, and a desire to take action in life.

*****

To love is to listen... To listen is to love.

*****

Empathic listening often shifts the responsibility for change from
the listener to the one who is sharing his concerns and at the
same time assures him that "I do not have to do this alone."

*****

Listening is more than a physical act between two people.
It is a sense of genuinely *being with* a person to the point of
making contact with one another's heart, spirit, and soul—
the essence of who we are.

*****

*Soul work is living the kind of life which
transcends doing and focuses us upon simply being.*

*****

Allowing others to get in touch with and express their pain is
the first and most crucial step in helping them to understand it,
shake hands with it, diffuse it, heal it, and learn from it. Now we
may begin to realize that our pain can be like a friend who is
trying to tell us something important about how we are living our
life. It moves us towards growth and those elusive things called
change and acceptance.

*****

Emotions such as hurt, anger, fear, and guilt that are
repressed, denied, minimized, rationalized, or suppressed are like a

time bomb waiting to go off. Listening to another's feelings helps to diffuse the intensity and encourages healthy forms of understanding and expression.

*****

When we are able to help others shift from *THINKING* or ruminating upon a struggle to *VERBALIZING* their thoughts and feelings, we have brought them closer to the real concerns and some possible solutions.

*****

Encouraging another to *TALK* about a problem rather than merely *think* about the issue is like sitting in the box seats instead of the bleachers at a baseball game. Up close the game takes on a totally different perspective. Things look and feel different. We experience them in a new light. It is not that the cheap seats are bad, but the good ones often put us more in the game.

I had the opportunity to take fifty high school boys to a professional basketball game one winter evening. As with most sizable groups, our location in the arena was in the nosebleed seats—so high up and far away that one was susceptible to altitude problems. The players looked very small and, unless one knew them well, it was difficult to recognize who was in the game. Reading the names on their backs was an impossibility. I remember rising to my feet and cheering a shot that looked sure to go in for our team, only to have it go over the entire backboard! A bit embarrassing...

Due to the sparse attendance most of the ushers went off duty at halftime and it was suggested that we move to a better location. Our new seats were in row number four, behind the basket. Wow, what a difference! We could hear the grunting of the players and the squeaking of their shoes, feel their pounding footsteps as they flew up and down the court, and see on their faces the look of determination as they fought for a rebound. It was as if we were at two different games. Like our new seats, good listeners can put us more in the game.

*****

Remember all of those times you went to the same place (like grandmom's) with your parents as a youngster? Then you got your license and the time came for you to drive there by yourself.

"How do I get there, Mom?" you asked.

"Why Honey, you've been there a hundred times and you don't remember?" she would reply.

There is a huge difference between driving a car and being a passenger. Such is often the difference between verbalizing a thought and keeping it to yourself. When you open up and talk about what is troubling you, it's as if you have just moved from the passenger seat to become the driver behind the wheel.

*****

Listening is the glue which bonds a relationship.

*****

Having the freedom to express our deepest desires, dreams, and thoughts—no matter how irrational or intimate—is a most liberating and humanizing experience.

*****

A listening ear may quiet a troubled heart.

*****

A listening and responsive ear is an invitation to grow.

*****

Listening is a kind of emotional hand holding which says,
"Even though I cannot take away your pain...
...I will *go into* your pain with you."
"Even though I cannot take away your hurt...
...I will *share* your hurt with you."
"Even though I cannot always be with you...
...*here, take my hand—today.*"

*****

Fear is the lock which keeps many of us from risking, changing, or becoming our best selves. Another's ear is often the key to opening the many rooms of our heart, life, and dreams. The love and listening of others helps to ease our fears and encourages us to move forward.

*****

The caring and listening ear of another helps us to redirect our life's energy towards becoming our best selves.

*****

The therapy and healing of listening is often of more value to the one who does the listening than it is to the one who talks. For it is in listening to another that we are *compelled* to listen to ourselves. The issues of our own life sometimes come floating or flying into our own being and force us to look at them once again. With each examination comes more dissipation of the pain and greater understanding and acceptance of what was... and is.

How many of us can realistically say that we have had at least one significant other who unconditionally and lovingly listened to us on a regular basis? Is it any coincidence that for the many who did not receive this kind of listening earlier in their life that they now find it difficult to give and listen to others?

Each time I get to this point in a presentation I ask for a show of hands of those who felt that they had someone who truly listened to and demonstrated listening for them while growing up. On the average, 10-20% say yes, they did have such a person. Never have I had more than half say they had such listeners. Once I had one out of twenty participants raise his hand!

*****

It seems that at the moment of birth, we were destined to have as our primary focus a desire to be heard. We spend much of our lives attempting to have others hear us, with little regard or awareness of also being a good listener to another. And by the way, it is often as much by our actions as it is through our words that we vie for attention!

*****

For many of us work is perhaps the most distasteful of all four-letter words. To listen is to *work*. To listen is to *love*. Giving

26

advice is a lot easier. I think I'll just stick to that!

*****

It often puzzles me that there is not more of Jesus's dialogue in the New Testament. Could one reason be that He spent most of His ministry hearing where people were in their lives before, or instead of, telling them what to do or who they could become? He seemed to value quite highly making choices and decisions from within one's own heart and soul, and thus, His nonjudgmental caring ear became a guiding force in their lives.

*****

Jesus humbled Himself before others and demonstrated his deep sense of caring and respect by washing their feet.

By *being with* and interested in another we follow His example.

*****

Jesus "knew their heart" is a familiar declaration which seems to imply some mystical or supernatural knowledge of a person's situation. Actually, it probably had as much to do with His deep caring and sensitivity to people that enabled Him to understand their plight on an intensely human level. He heard their concerns, conflicts, and feelings. And thus, He *"knew their heart."*

*****

"Everybody's talking around me...I don't hear a word they're saying...Only the echoes of my mind," are the lyrics in a song from a popular 1960s movie. It so vividly describes the greatest reason that we often lack the ability to listen to others. Our personal *garbage* often gets in the way.

It's tough to hear the many expressions from those around us when so much continues to reverberate within.

*****

The *garbage* in our lives that keeps us from effectively hearing another must be dealt with and taken out as regularly as the trash in our house. Until we recognize this, we will continue to listen with distorted ears, ears that hear what they want to hear, ears that color and misinterpret the words of others, ears that become more consumed with what is going on inside the listener's own head than within that of the speaker.

*****

In simple terms we function in two primary modes—either the *cognitive* or the *affective* domain. We spend much of our time processing in the cognitive or thinking part of our brain. A good listener can help a person to do some work in the affective or feeling realm. While the cognitive is important, the affective area is equally vital.

We need to become more at home with our feeling life.

*****

Our primary sex organs are located in four basic areas:
our heart, our eyes, our ears, and our souls.
Talking eye to eye, ear to ear, heart to heart, and soul to soul
is among life's most intimate encounters.

*****

"I can't tell you how much I appreciate your spending some time with me. I've never really shared these things before. You really listened to me," are words that have occasionally been directed to me (and I'm sure to you) and which never fail to arouse some potent feelings.

Inside I felt very pleased, flattered, and encouraged that you could share these thoughts and feelings with me. I am a bit disheartened that there has never been nor currently is a person who can be that listener for you. I am saddened that you have missed so much by never opening up like that previously in your life. I hope this is a beginning for you...

*****

As consumers and decision makers, we have had the opportunity to become more and more selective. If not a choice of fifty TV programs to watch, then it is the decision of which fast food emporium to pick. Our listening ability is also quite selective. Namely, *we often hear what we want or choose to hear.*

*****

Does this little saying summarize the listening
and understanding dilemma or what?!?

"I Know That You Believe You Understand What You Think I Said, But I Am Not Sure You Realize That What You Heard Is Not What I Meant..."

(EXACTLY!)

"That's not what I said *or* meant" are sentiments uttered on a regular basis. Either we heard only parts, read into the portions we did hear, or made another of our endless assumptions. Please check at regular intervals to insure that you have heard accurately.

> The following phrases can be quite helpful:
> "Is this what you mean..?"
> "Let me make sure I understand this...,"
> "In other words, you are saying...,"
> "Time out, I think I missed something...,"
> or "Let's back up for a moment. I want to make sure I heard you correctly!"

*****

A social work student stopped by my office one day and with a look of exasperation said to me, "I'm not really helping anyone at my internship in this agency. All I can really do is *just listen* to these kids. I can't really help them!" At this instant I felt my face flush, temperature rise, and was close to the point of strangulation! With clenched teeth, I struggled out with a restrained, "all you can really do is *just listen*!?!"

I took a deep breath and proceeded to have a rather stimulating discussion with my student. It seems that after four years of being saturated with lectures centered around the gospel of listening as a key to helping others, she, like most of us, wanted to be able to give some magical solutions to their problems. We all wish we could just fix things, don't we?

*****

If I could remove one word from a dictionary to help us become better listeners it would be "WHY??" Being asked "why" not only serves to put another into a corner or on the defensive but also prematurely begs an answer from a person who is either unable to, incapable of, or not ready to supply. It smacks of analysis and forces the speaker back into his head. Keep him in his heart as much as possible and then begin to put the two together.

30

LISTEN

When I ask you to listen to me and you start giving advice, you have not done what I asked.

When I ask you to listen to me and you begin to tell me why I shouldn't feel that way, you are trampling on my feelings.

When I ask you to listen to me and you feel you have to do something to solve my problem, you have failed me, strange as that may seem.

Listen! All I ask is that you listen.

Not talk or do... just hear me.

Advice is cheap: 50 cents will get you both Dear Abby and Billy Graham in the same newspaper.

And I can do for myself; I'm not helpless.

Maybe discouraged and faltering, but not helpless.

When you do something for me that I can and need to do for myself, you contribute to my fear and weakness.

But when you accept as a simple fact that I do feel what I feel, no matter how irrational, then I can quit trying to convince you and get about the business of understanding what's behind this irrational feeling.

And when that's clear, the answers are obvious, and I don't need advice. Irrational feelings make sense when we understand what's behind them.

Perhaps that's why prayer works, sometimes, for some people because God is mute, and He doesn't give advice or try to fix things. He just listens and lets you work it out for yourself.

So, please listen and just hear me.

And, if you want to talk, wait a minute for your turn;

and I'll listen to you...

Anonymous

*****

The end result of listening to another is not necessarily that she will feel better or be over her pain. Indeed, because your thoughtful listening encouraged and invited her to look more closely at her life, she may be closer to her hurt and feel it more intensely. This is often the true beginning of the healing process. It might, and probably will, hurt even more for awhile. Having built up for such a long period of time, once contacted, this pain comes screaming at us.

It may help to buy some extra tissues.

*****

We generally have two choices when it comes to pain and conflict in our lives. We either choose (consciously or unconsciously) to push it down, defend against, rationalize and minimize it—or we can plod through it.

We basically can take the pain in two forms:

(1) Holding the pain in and allowing it to constantly affect and modify our lives, relationships, and physical wellbeing, or

(2) Choosing to deal with the pain by owning it, experiencing it, expressing it, understanding it, and allowing it to heal.

A good listener can certainly come in handy when it comes to accessing and coping with hurt and pain.

*****

Many of our conversations and relationships are strikingly similar to placing two radios or TV sets face to face, turning them on and allowing them to play unattended. There could be a lot of good stuff coming out of them but who could prove or know it?

*****

Life is made up of some rather trivial and mundane daily tasks; however, a good dose of listening can inject stimulation into the most ordinary of days. When two minds, hearts, and souls genuinely meet—no matter how short the time—we are energized and encouraged to live our lives more fully for that moment and that day.

SLOW ME DOWN LORD

Slow me down, Lord!

Ease the pounding of my heart

By the quieting of my mind.

Steady my harried pace

With a vision of the eternal reach of time.

Give me, amidst the confusion of my day,

The calmness of the everlasting hills.

Break the tensions of my nerves

With the soothing music of the singing streams that live in my memory.

Help me to know the magical restoring power of sleep.

Teach me the art of taking minute vacations of slowing down

to look at a flower;

to chat with an old friend or make a new one;

to pat a stray dog;

to watch a spider build a web;

to smile at a child;

or to read a few lines from a good book.

Remind me each day that the race is not always to the swift;

That there is more to life than increasing its speed.

Let me look upward

Into the branches of the towering oak

And know that it grew great and strong

Because it grew slowly and well.

Slow me down, Lord,

And inspire me to send my roots deep

Into the soil of life's enduring values

That I may grow toward the stars

Of my greater destiny.

"The Art of Living" By Wilferd A. Peterson

*****

Look Out, Listeners! A healthy dose of listening not only has the ability to change the speaker but just might affect the listener too! Perhaps I need to make some of the same changes he does!!

*****

Our battles in life are largely fought in the common "arenas" of sex, finances, careers, grade point averages, and a host of others. Into these arenas we pour the true and lasting issues of our life such as low self worth, feelings of inadequacy, control, perfectionism, the need to be liked by everyone, etc.

It is a rather liberating experience when a listener can break through the outward problem to the authentic issue with which we are struggling! For it is often not sex, finances, careers, or grade points that are the real problems; but, rather, one of these lifelong issues. A sensitive ear can often sift through the smoke screen to what is really going on.

*****

The more I listen, the more I realize just how much I am <u>not</u> listening. Sounds like double talk, doesn't it? Yet it is precisely in becoming aware of my times of *non-listening* that I will really *begin* to become a better listener. The people who concern me the most are those that think they are good listeners but in fact are not. They not only miss a lot but feel no need to work on their listening skills.

*****

You would think if there was any place in this world that we could be listened to, cared about, and unconditionally accepted, it would be down at the corner church. Unfortunately we will probably find more of that going on at the corner bar. Why was it that when I so desperately needed to talk, I was met with a concerned look and the short response of "I'll pray for you," or "I'll be thinking about you"?

Wait, don't you see? I do not just want to be prayed for, but also need so much for you to hear my pain... *Now*.

34

It's much easier and more comfortable though to say "I'll pray for you" and then move on than to stay and listen for awhile.

*****

I encountered a most interesting irony of life while working for the local alcoholism treatment center. I was involved with statewide prevention activities which involved planning and training workshops on a small-group basis. The twist came when I realized that these people, many of whom knew very little about me, listened more intently and with greater interest and concern than those people with whom I worshipped regularly at church.

My fellow group members dared to broach topics and issues in my life which were quite personal and literally screaming to be addressed.

Why weren't my close friends able do the same thing for me?

*****

There are certainly times when one may need the assistance of a professional counselor, yet too often we sell ourselves short on the therapeutic and healing power of our own ears in helping one another.

*****

Nothing is more exhilarating than being affirmed as a person of value and worth. There is no better way to bestow this affirmation than by the awesome power of our listening ears, eyes, mind, and heart.

*****

The dissonance of hearing a French horn played a trifle off key during a symphony performance is highly analogous to the disconcerted feelings one experiences when being listened to by a person whose perception is slightly distorted. They just cannot seem to finely tune into us. And what they think they are hearing is off kilter or a bit skewed from what we are actually trying to say. How frustrating!

*****

In an age when practically any type of pill or drug is available

35

to help us anesthetize our pain, it helps me to remember that we can still quiet our pain from within. The only outside stimulus needed is that of a good listener.

It saddened me deeply to see how many of my students would forego expressing their inner selves and instead use alcohol or other drugs on a regular basis to deal with their issues. Although this may serve to help deaden or divert the pain, it will not stop it. It remains alive and active inside, coloring the sense of our world and our relationships, modifying our behavior, and affecting everything we do.

*****

A good listener brings sunshine to the stormiest of days.

*****

In this era of assertiveness and people's rights, doing battle with others for actions and attitudes that we do not like in them is a regular occurrence. And speaking of rights, what about the way we must *earn* the right to confront another?

Please do not confront me until you have first tried to hear and understand me. With a proven track record of listening and caring, I can hear much better your concerns about my way of life. However, without the element of compassion, your confrontation becomes an attack on my values and personhood. With concern and understanding, it becomes an invitation and challenge to reflect upon my life more closely and to consider making changes.

*****

A frequent question asked of me is "How do I make or improve my friendships?" In one word I respond, *"Listen."*

*****

Many of the most charming, considerate, and attractive people I know would win few beauty contests. Their genuine and infectious smiles, looks of acceptance, and listening ears are magnetically appealing. Their very countenance says to me, "I hear you, I understand you, I feel with you, I value you."

"You're beautiful."

THE FRIEND WHO JUST STANDS BY

When trouble comes your soul to try

You love the friend who just stands by

Perhaps there's nothing he can do

The thing is strictly up to you

For there are troubles all your own

And paths the soul must tread alone

Times when love can't smooth the road

Nor friendship lift the heavy load

But just to feel you have a friend

Who will stand by until the end

Whose sympathy through all endures

Whose warm hand clasp is always yours

It helps somehow to pull you through

Although there's nothing he can do

And so with fervent heart we cry

God Bless the friend who just stands by

Author Unknown

I can never seem to hear God talking to me.
I wish I knew what He was trying to say to me.
Have you quieted your mind long enough
to listen to His eternal voice?

*****

My husband (my wife, my child, my student, my friend, my
_____) never talks to me. He's got to be feeling a lot inside
but he just won't open up. What can I do?

Have you been quiet long enough to hear what he perhaps
cannot or does not know how to express? Have you refrained from
the urge to fill the air with words in order to allow him to release a
few of his own?

*****

Loneliness is perhaps the most prevalent and cruelest of all
the maladies in our hurting world. A listening ear is among the
most potent healers of this isolation.

*****

Sally was a young mother of a very vibrant and intelligent
daughter named Francie. Francie, having read the many warnings
and heard the numerous stories about artificial sweeteners
possibly causing cancer, regularly watched with concern and fear
as her mother drank diet cola. One day as her mother sipped on a
diet cola, Francie abruptly stated, "Mom, I don't want you to die!"

"What are you talking about, Francie?" Sally replied.

"If you drink any more of that cola you'll die from cancer,"
Francie said. Sally had a quick choice to make. Sally thought "do I
simply laugh and tell her how silly she is _or_ do I try and hear
what she is *really* trying to communicate to me?" Diet cola was
not the issue. Francie's real thinking was, "I want to know you
will always be here, Mommy. I love you and need you."

Being a wise mother and social worker, Sally chose the latter
option. She has learned the value and importance of looking
beyond the words or what *seemed* to be the obvious.

Nice work, Sally.

"And I Have to Follow Him?!?"

The one-hour drive from the conference center to my home seemed forever; endless, perhaps, because of the internal dialogue I was using to beat myself up. I'm sure none of you know anything about self-inflicted verbal assaults. Your "self talk" is always positive, uplifting, and nurturing, right?

Let me set the scene. I was working all week with one hundred colleagues in a rather intensive training. That afternoon we participated in the most stimulating workshop of the week, led by the best of a lineup of several excellent presenters. He was so good the participants asked to postpone dinner in order to keep going! I had never heard of such a request.

Much of that day, on the evening drive home, and now at my house, I was feeling increasingly anxious, fearful, and inadequate. "How come?" you ask. Well, guess who the next speaker was the entire following morning? Moi! It didn't matter that I was excited about the topic and the chance to present it at this conference. It didn't matter that it was a talk I had given hundreds of times before. It didn't matter that the audience was a group of very upbeat, involved, and open people.

What mattered was that my usual feelings of being a bit nervous (quite normal, mind you) were exacerbated tenfold! These were not only colleagues (who are sometimes a more difficult group to speak to), but my topic seemed much less interesting and my presentation skills much less dynamic than the person preceding me. I kept thinking, "How can I

39

possibly equal what he did? What can I do to spice up my talk and reach this group like he did?"

At home that evening I did what I often do when I am feeling stressed out. I acted a tad edgy, appeared a trifle preoccupied, and said everything was "fine!" Some of you can relate to this just a little bit, can't you?

After looking at my notes and rearranging a few lines for the umpteenth time, I turned in for the evening. As I lay there in bed feeling overwhelmed about what was to happen in just ten short hours, I heard Sue's gentle voice asking if everything was okay.

As if automatically, I began to recite "Yeah, sure, everything's o..." On the outside the words flowed. Inside, they seemed to choke. I caught myself midstream and feebly mumbled, "Well, ah, actually I..."

What if I get the "Oh Steve, you shouldn't be worried—Why you've done it hundreds of times before—I'm sure it will go just fine response? Should I really tell her everything I was feeling? It's not all completely rational. This isn't life or death, and it's not as important as you are making it out to be. Lighten up man!"

"Remember that you and the other speaker are two very different people. He's good at what he does, and you're good at what you do. The message you have for them is important too. They are a fun and supportive group. It's okay to be nervous. And besides, so what if you make a mistake or they are not as receptive to you? Does that mean you are less than or not capable?

"Isn't life a lot more to you than your work?"

It is amazing how much stuff can go through one's mind

in such a short period of time. The tape is always cued up in our head and ready to start playing on command. Sometimes it's as soft as a three-piece ensemble. Other times it reverberates like the Ohio State Marching Band!

Well, here goes...

"Sue, I guess I'm kinda scared about my talk tomorrow. I..." (and I went on with the story). Even though it was dark, I could sense Sue's concern. I also felt a slight hesitation and pause, as if she was gently retrieving to her lips the already spoken words, "But Steve, you shouldn't feel..." and in turn replacing them with the unspoken, yet clear message, "Keep talking, Steve..."

I babbled for about ten minutes after which she responded with "I can see this whole thing really has you worked up. Talk to me some more about it." A few moments later, having the benefit of Sue's unconditional ears and listening to what was really on my heart, I got to the root of what was bothering me, hugged her in thanks, and shortly fell asleep.

Well-rested and with renewed enthusiasm for the workshop, I was on my way to the conference. The three-hour presentation flew by... or should I say "flowed by?" It felt like the best talk I had ever given. They even laughed more loudly than usual at the dumb jokes I tell. There was a connection between the group and me.

It is amazing what a little old fashioned, nonjudgmental you-can-tell-me-anything-because-I-care-about-you listening will do for a person's spirit.

What was the topic of this little workshop you may be wondering? Why, what else? *LISTENING,* of course!

"The most important things are the hardest things to say.

"They are things that you get ashamed of, because words diminish them. Words shrink things that seem limitless when they were in your head to no more than living size when they're brought out.

"But it's more than that, isn't it? The most important things lie too close to wherever your secret heart is buried, like landmarks to a treasure your enemies would like to steal away.

"And you may make revelations that cost you dearly only to have people look at you in a funny way, not understanding what you've said at all, or why you thought it was so important that you almost cried while you were saying it.

"That's the worst, I think. When the secret stays locked within not for want of a teller but for the want of an understanding ear."

Stephen King, *"Different Body"* (The Body)

*****

Stop for a minute. Reflect upon this next thought. As you continue to read and process these writings are you still saying, "I wish _____ (insert favorite person's name!) were reading this book? What a difference this could make for him. Every other paragraph seems to be written just for him."

Now, can you bring these ideas back into your world and ask the question "How can I change? Maybe I should just concern myself with what I can do with this information. Changing me is difficult enough."

What a convenient way to avoid examining my own life and listening habits by looking at the faults or shortcomings of another!

*****

The way we listen or do not listen is very much a product of who we were and who we have become. We have been influenced by a variety of life-shaping forces such as our parents, teachers, family, friends, and coaches along with the host of expectations and feelings each has or perhaps more powerfully, what *we have perceived* each person has for us. If you grew up with few positive models for healthy relationships and listening skills, then you may need to work even harder in these areas to improve.

*****

Proverbs 23:7 states that *"for as a man thinketh in his heart so is he.."* We are constantly projecting our feelings, thoughts, fears, conflicts, desires, needs, and values in spite of how exquisitely we attempt or are able to hide them.

The good listener can begin to read these non-verbal messages such as a facial expression that does not match a feeling being discussed or the way a person walks when he is angry. In spite of ourselves, we are constantly giving off messages about how we feel and who we are. The non-verbal simply does not lie!

Caring and perceptive listeners are willing and able to pick up on these indicators and gently work them into the conversation.

*****

A lint trap serves an important function in a clothes dryer. If not cleaned out with regularity, it will accumulate an abundance of lint which reduces the dryer's efficiency and could even cause a fire! Have you checked your own filter lately?

I wonder what is keeping you from hearing?
*****

It would be great if we could actually get into the bodies of others and walk around in them for awhile. To live, eat, breathe, sleep, work, play, cry, and laugh with them would surely give us a perspective into their lives that would otherwise have never been revealed to us.

Perhaps the best we can truly hope for is to begin hearing less through our own ears and more *as if* we were in their situation.

That's real empathy in action.
*****

When two or more people look at a situation—discuss it, argue it, dissect it, walk around it, feel it, examine it, and wonder about how it might be changed or improved—somehow the issue comes out appearing quite different from when it was first encountered—especially by only one's self.
*****

I could not believe the openness I encountered at the hair styling shop. It was the first time for getting my hair cut in a place that served both men and women. When entering a men's barber shop, the air is filled with heated discussions of the ninth inning of last night's game or of tips on finding the busiest fishing holes.

Spend some time in a beauty salon and you are likely to hear a person's concern about a family member, excitement over an upcoming event, or how they are feeling about most anything. It's no wonder that there are probably more hairdressers and stylists in a town than pastors and counselors! The therapy taking place in a women's beauty salon is phenomenal. You will find both ready talkers and willing listeners. Any topic seems to be fair game.

There are times when my barber Darcy or I could have billed each other for a counseling session. The haircut was incidental. I call it "cut and counsel" or "clip and chat." Everyone should be so blessed with a hair care professional as wise, compassionate, and adept at listening as mine.

She really ought to charge more!

*****

A familiar saying comes to mind that states:

"It seems to be no coincidence that God gave to man two ears and only one mouth, ears that would stay open and a mouth that could close."

An excellent thought indeed with an added point to ponder.

How do you *open* or *close* your ears to those around you?

*****

When presenting this topic to various groups, one assignment I invariably give is for participants to list and describe the attributes of their best friends. Inevitably the top items include the following:

(1) they care about me

(2) I can trust them

(3) they accept me as I am (unconditionally)

(4) they try to and do understand me, and

(5) they value me.

As these traits are shared and discussed the question is posed:

"How could you best sum up these factors?"

What is their most common conclusion?

"They *LISTEN* to me."

The group members' eyes widen, smiles broaden, and heads begin to nod. On their lips and in their minds I can hear them quietly repeat,

"They *LISTEN* to me. That's what it is! They *LISTEN* to me..."

*****

What a great feeling overwhelms listeners when they sense and ultimately experience a "lightbulb" or "ah ha!" moment with another. This is the kind of insight which sheds new light on an old issue or causes us to look at something from a fresh perspective. It is often the impetus that moves us towards change.

Have you had any lightbulb experiences lately? I hope so...

What were they? Go tell someone about them!

*****

The message of Jesus calls us to love others and to love our neighbors as ourselves. To love and listen to another takes a lot of energy. What are you doing to become healthier and more energetic in order to better love and listen to your world? Do you take care of yourself physically?

*****

The foundation of trust is formed and strengthened by active and honest sharing *and* listening to each other. Trust leads to openness. Openness leads to trust.

Listening makes and completes this cycle.

*****

Much of our pain and fear is rooted in the life-shaping experiences we are exposed to and involved in throughout our life. Remember the fear of going into a dark basement at age five? It is a liberating feeling to know that we may feel that same sense of fear at age 30, 40, 50, etc. and that another person may allow us the freedom to experience and express it.

*****

Listening is one of the most creative and life-enhancing forces in all of our world. It can help create a particular mood, feeling, positive thought, healthy relationship, and bond with another human being.

*****

To "hear" as opposed to "listen" are two quite different activities. In listening we hear with *thoughtful attention* and with a *conscious effort* rather than merely taking in the sounds and words around us.

Many of us simply *Hear* rather than actively *Listen*.

"Listen to all the conversations of our world, those between nations as well as those between couples. They are for the most part dialogues of the deaf.

"Exceedingly few exchanges of viewpoints manifest a real desire to understand the other person....

"No one can find a full life without feeling understood at least by one person. Misunderstood, he loses his self-confidence, he loses his faith in life, or even in God.

"Here is an even greater mystery: no one comes to know himself [completely] through introspection, or in the solitude of his personal diary.

"He who would see himself clearly must open up to a confidant freely chosen and worthy of such trust. It may be a friend just as easily as a doctor; it may also be one's marital partner."

"To Understand Each Other" By Paul Tournier

*****

The ultimate act of a good listener is in making every effort to direct or redirect the speaker along the pathway that would be in *her* best interest and not where the listener may need to take it for his own benefit, comfort level, agenda, or sense of control. This often calls for a great deal of self awareness and discipline!

*****

Listening is often described as a lost art.

My question is, "Was it ever a 'developed art' in the first place?" This is similar to our declaration that juvenile delinquents and criminals must be rehabilitated. How many of them ever had the opportunity to first be "habilitated?"

You cannot *"re"* anything unless there was first something there with which to begin. Let's begin from the beginning.

*****

The very contour of our ears with their large cone-shaped receptors (some bigger than others!) seem to quietly say to our world "talk to me."

Unfortunately, our face and body speak more loudly to another by their message of "I don't really want to hear you."

*****

The eyes can warm the coldest of hearts.

*****

James 1:19 says, "...let every man be swift to hear, slow to speak..."

God, help the initial reaction to my world to be that of a ready listener who tries to hear and understand *before* I react or respond.

*****

Wise King Solomon in Proverbs 18:13 tells us that *"he that answereth a matter before he heareth it, it is folly and shame unto him."* Please don't finish my sentences for me or continually assume to know what I am about to say. I hope that I will be more sensitive to how I often cut off another's thoughts and that I might become more tolerant of those who do it to me.

I take it so personally.

*****

Who usually finishes first at your meals? Are they fast eaters and good listeners? Are they avid talkers and slow eaters? We can observe our daily routines to check our listening quotient.

It struck me one day while eating a meal with friends that I had a plate covered with food as they were finishing their last spoonful. I am usually a pretty fast eater. I guess I really needed to talk this day.

Thanks for listening, good friends.

*****

The concept that we are "whole persons" is permeating our consciousness and our bookstores. Lest we get completely caught up in the zest to fulfill our needs in all of these whole-person dimensions, can we keep as our watchword *balance*?

There is a fine line between giving and getting; and just as surely as we are encouraged to listen to others, we also have a need to be heard. The mark of a healthy person is their quest for balance in all things.

*****

A major dilemma for the person who becomes the all-giving, all-caring listener is "Who listens to the listener when the listener needs to be listened to?"

And, does the listener even recognize her own need to be listened to?"

Sometimes always being the caring listener is a convenient way for us to not look at and deal with our own life. Constantly reaching out keeps us from ever looking within. It's hard to hear ourselves when we keep so busy doing for and working on other peoples' problems.

*****

The Golden Rule seems so appropriate when considering this entire area. How exciting it would be if we indeed did:

"Listen unto others as we would want them to listen unto us!"

*****

A familiar prayer we hear or offer each week at church or by our bedside is "Lord, please meet our needs."

The question I must ask is, "Do we even know, recognize, or care to admit what our specific needs are?"

Surely God does know our needs, but perhaps He would like us to more actively become aware of them, to own them, to verbalize them, to challenge them, to make friends with them, and to deal with them.

Good listeners can help here.

*****

Somehow we have developed the notion that our *not being listened to* is not quite the same as our *not listening to another,* or that the exhilaration we feel after having been listened to is not strikingly similar to the positive feelings the speaker experiences when we listen to them.

Think again.

*****

Genuine Listening is art in its highest form.

*****

There are certain people to whom we find it nearly impossible to listen. The reasons are as infinite as there are people and personalities. Consider a few in the following list... (from your point of view!)

> attractive/unattractive
> rich/poor
> unappealing/appealing
> slow talker/fast talker
> our religion/a different religion
> says nothing/says too much
> arrogant/humble
> male/female
> black/white

young/old

native/foreign

same status/different status

interesting/boring

good person/bad person

educated/uneducated

(you can add one or two here!) _____

Perhaps the greatest factor of all is that they remind us in some conscious or unconscious way (personality, looks, voice tone, attitude, name, etc.) of someone we know. They may have brought up something from within us that hits too close to home.

I recall my wife Sue, a teacher, coming home one afternoon exasperated. "It's only the second day of the school year and already there is one student I really don't like at all! He just rubs me the wrong way," she said.

To her credit, by the end of the week she said to me, "It's really been bugging me that I have these feelings about this student. Then it came to me. There's something about him which reminds me of this one student I had a few years ago. No matter what I did to try to understand and get along with him, he just kept disrupting the class. Once I realized my reactions to this new student were more my problem than his, I have had a much better attitude about him. I needed to see and treat him for *who he is* and not *for the other student he reminded me of.*"

Good work, Sue! Teachers are often guilty of this. Many are quite notorious for doing it with siblings too. They expect the same things from the students and treat them in much the same way they did their older brother or sister. *Work at this, teachers!*

It's amazing to think of the many triggering forces that keep us from hearing another! This listening stuff can sure get involved!

*****

Do you still think listening is easy to cultivate and do most anytime? It's oftentimes as complicated as each different human being is complicated!

PLEASE HEAR WHAT I'M NOT SAYING
(Anonymous Poet)

Don't be fooled by me. Don't be fooled by the face I wear. For I wear a mask. I wear a thousand masks. Masks that I'm afraid to take off. And none of them are me.

Pretending is an art that is second nature to me, but don't be fooled. I give you the impression that I am secure—that all is sunny and unruffled with me, within as well as without.

That confidence is my name, and coolness is my game. The water's calm. I'm in command. I need no one. But don't believe me. Please.

My surface may be smooth, but my surface is my mask—my very and every concealing mask. Beneath it dwells the real me: in confusion, fear, and loneliness.

But I hide this. I don't want anybody to know this. I panic at the thoughts of my weakness and the fear of being exposed. That's why I frantically create a mask to hide behind.

It is a nonchalant, sophisticated facade...to help me pretend...to shield me from the glance that knows. But such a glance is precisely my salvation—my only salvation. And I know it...that is if it is followed by acceptance...if it is followed by love. It is the only thing that can liberate me from myself...from my self-built prison walls...from the barriers that I so painstakingly erect.

It is the only thing that will assure me of what I can't assure myself...that I'm really worth something.

But I don't tell you this. I don't dare. I'm afraid to. I'm afraid that your glance will not be followed by acceptance. I'm afraid that your glance will not be followed by love. I'm afraid that you will think less of me. That you'll laugh and your laugh will kill me.

I'm afraid down deep that I'm nothing, that I'm just no good, and that you will see this and reject me.

So I play my game... with the facade of assurance without and a trembling child within. And so begins the parade of masks, the glittering but empty parade of masks.

And my life becomes a front.

I idly chatter to you in the suave tones of surface talk. I tell you everything that's really nothing and nothing that is everything of what is crying within me.

So when I'm going through my routine, do not be fooled by what I'm saying.

Please listen carefully and try to hear what I'm not saying, and what I'd like to be able to say, but what I can't say.

Honestly, I dislike the superficial game I'm playing, the superficial phony game. I'd really like to be genuine and spontaneous—and me.

But you've got to hold out your hand, even when that is the last thing I seem to want or need.

Only you can wipe away from my eyes that blank stare of the breathing dead.

Only you can call me into aliveness each time you're kind, gentle, and encouraging—each time you're soft and understanding because you really care. My heart begins to grow wings—very small wings, but wings.

53

With your sympathy, sensitivity, and your power of understanding, you can breathe life into me. I want you to know that. I want you to know how important you are to me. How you can be a creator of the person that is me if you choose to. *Please* choose to.

You alone can break down the wall behind which I tremble.

You alone can remove my mask.

You alone can release me from my show world of panic and uncertainty, from my lonely prison.

So don't pass me by. It will not be easy for you. A long conviction of worthlessness builds strong walls.

The nearer your approach to me, the blinder I may strike back. It's irrational, but despite what the book says about me, I'm irrational. I fight against the very thing I cry out for.

But I am told that love is stronger than strong walls. In this lies my hope. My only hope.

Please try to beat down those walls with firm but gentle hands, for a child is very sensitive.

Who am I you may wonder?

I am someone you know very well.

I pass you on the street.

I am sitting beside you.

I am every boy, and

I am every girl,

I am every man, and

I am every woman you meet.

*****

We know that our values and attitudes are shaped largely by our upbringing, parents and family, peers, the media, cultural norms, religious beliefs, and personal experiences. Of these factors, personal experience seems to be the most influential. All it takes is one look, one word, or one idea expressed by a speaker to trigger a memory bank of experiences, set of biases, or rush of feelings, and in turn, affect your attitude about the one talking or about the words that he speaks.

Is it no wonder that the daughter of an alcoholic who has negligible insight into her issues has such a tough time listening to a talk on alcoholism as a disease? Is it so hard to understand why a young man can not fully listen to his friend's struggles with a girlfriend when he himself has not fared very well in this area?

What are the attitudes you need to pound at and adjust? Are you willing to see how they interfere with your listening and understanding? And as I've heard it said, if you are not willing to do battle with your inflexible and harmful attitudes, then they will probably die about an hour after you do!

*****

The courage to go on with living and face one's difficulties as they come is what a listener often gives to another. And in dealing with our *present* struggles, we often develop the strength to resolve some of our *past* pain and the resources to take on those with which we may encounter in the *future*.

*****

Vacation time was often both a source of great pleasure as well as much consternation for me. The joy came in knowing what lay ahead at the ocean and boardwalk. The pain derived from the frustration of packing, loading, and leaving.

One summer I recall lugging what seemed to be an endless array of boxes, suitcases, and loose items to the car. I sarcastically asked my father, "Where am I going to sit—strapped to the roof of the car?" Needless to say, that flip remark did not go over real well!

55

What I deemed to be excess baggage often squelched the enthusiasm I had for the trip and vacation.

Excess baggage accompanies our personal journey also. From the moment we were born, the packing begins. It ranges from small handbags to 500-lb. trunks. And just because we say we no longer have them does not mean they are gone. Out of sight is not necessarily out of mind. They are still there.

What a liberating experience it is to have someone remove a few suitcases by their listening ears! How many boxes are you holding right now? Who in your life might you care to help lighten the load?

When someone listens to us it's as if we are better able to discard another suitcase from our life, lighten the luggage we have to carry, and most of all, make the trip more enjoyable.

*****

I am ever more thankful each day that my parents made attempts, successful or not, at trying to hear and understand me. Their sensitivity and valuing of others had a profound influence on me. For so many years it was my prayer, plea, and frustration with God that caused me to ask, "Why, God, do I have to be so sensitive?"

Now I say, "Thank you, God, for developing this in me through You and my parents so that I might better listen to myself and others. I look at those who cannot even feel or touch another and I hurt for them. What so often seemed to be a curse in my life has begun to become a strength."

Don't be afraid to release your own untapped reservoir of compassion and sensitivity.

*****

A good listener not only hears where a person is...
...but senses who they may become.

*****

So often the answers to our questions lie partly or wholly within our being. A good listener can be the catalyst in bringing us closer to touching these solutions and alternatives.

*****

The creative energy that goes into and becomes
stimulated by building a house, painting a picture,
styling a song, or planting a garden is phenomenal.
So is the energy in our intimate listening relationships.

*****

In the Gospel of Luke, chapter eighteen, infants were brought to Jesus to be touched and blessed. When the disciples saw this they told the mothers to take their children away. In that time and culture, children were often not looked upon or valued as people. They were second class citizens. Jesus immediately called the children to him—picking them up, touching them, and blessing them.

And who says kids are not people too and that they should be seen and *not* heard? Listen to children—not only because by doing so we are helping to guide them to become healthy adults, but also because they can teach us so much about our own life.

They are like mirrors to us if we will only look and listen. They tap into and teach us about our own fears, hopes, expectations, and feelings. They often show us parts of ourselves that we have forgotten, lost touch with, not wanted to acknowledge, or have never fully resolved.

*****

Not listening to our children and young people plants the seeds for them to begin accumulating the garbage in their lives with all of its emotional bondage. Being a "good boy" or "good girl" by not expressing anger, hurt, or pain is a sure ticket for insuring that they too will feed on the endless diet of approval from others and ride the merry-go-round of emotional debt. Allow and encourage in them the freedom to feel.

*****

Approval is a distant second cousin to self-acceptance. Without ever feeling that sense of unconditional acceptance from a significant other and in turn a sense of personal "O.K.ness," we strive aimlessly and relentlessly for the approval of anyone and often everyone around us.

One or two compassionate listeners early in our lives could have done wonders for this critical period of development. Be encouraged, however, for it can begin taking place right *now*!

*****

In my office on a table next to the desk resides a tiny little bird who slides rhythmically down and around a pole to one of eight landing spots alternately labeled "yes" or "no."

On occasion, when a client, student, or friend seems stuck for an answer and the situation is appropriate, we start the bird on his journey to an answer. This is often enough to break the ice, end the stalemate, help the person to get untracked and moving towards discovering a solution.

The sad thing is that many of us make decisions based on less reliable sources than the little bird in my office. If only they could have talked to someone who would think and feel with them and possibly walk and talk them through a few of the various alternatives and choices.

*****

A good listener holds a figurative mirror up to the speaker so that she can better see and hear what she is feeling, thinking, and doing. Life's picture becomes more clear, defined, and focused.

*****

"Give a hungry man a fish and he will eat for a day. Teach him to fish and he will eat for a lifetime." This old adage gets to the heart of what a good listener can be for another.

Give advice or tell a person how to live and you may help him for a day. Be a listener to another as he works to get in touch with his issues, struggles, and choices and you help him to develop the resources to deal with any future pain and concerns.

You have helped him for a lifetime.

*****

58

The Letter

The further along in the letter I read, the more the tears began to well up. "Where is all of this coming from?" I wondered as I feebly finished the final lines. Only hours before I had read this same letter, attaching little emotion to its contents. But this time it felt much different—and in addition, I was reading the letter in front of my social work class. What must they be thinking? Is Steve losing it or what?

My mom sent the letter describing my dad's surprise retirement luncheon. What he thought would be a small gathering of a few close colleagues turned into a major celebration with more than one hundred co-workers from around the state of New Jersey! These were all men and women who had been touched in some way by my dad's life. Needless to say, my dad was overwhelmed by this outpouring of affection and love.

My students were exploring possible careers and what it might be like to work in the real world. Reading the letter about my dad's job seemed to be a nice lead into a discussion of the meaning and purpose of our life's vocation. As I heard myself say the actual words I moved closer to the depth of feeling that my mom must have been experiencing when she wrote them. I also began to understand their impact upon me.

It was not simply a factual description about a two-hour period of time in my dad's life. It wasn't just a cute little story about his retirement party and new gold watch. It was more about *who my dad was*; my relationship to him; the miles that separated us; his getting older; and the inevitable changes in store for him, my mom, and our family. It was a lot of father and son stuff too.

Taking the words from the the paper and giving them a voice forged a connection between my head and my heart. Oh, and by the way, everyone in class that day received an "A" in listening.

Thanks, gang. Once again your listening taught the teacher!

*****

A good way to have a successful interview or land a job is by being a good listener and, when appropriate, picking up on the feelings, thoughts, and ideas of the interviewer. As you leave, the interviewer might not put their finger specifically on your listening skills but may be heard to say "There's just something I like about that person. She seemed so mature, aware, understanding, and intelligent." You're hired!

*****

When we listen to and challenge those who are sharing, we begin to teach them a *life skill*, namely, to listen to and challenge *themselves* more regularly and <u>on</u> <u>their</u> <u>own</u>.

*****

Frequently while listening to another I have been on the brink of beginning my sermon on how he ought to live his life. Or I begin telling him exactly how he is feeling. (This is not to say there aren't times to be more directive, give feedback or suggestions, etc.). This especially occurs when I am asked to give a little advice to someone. "Why he needs my wonderful expertise," I think.

If asked such a question, a reflex reaction causes me to immediately bring the most convenient hand to my lips, clear my throat, or mumble as he keeps talking. Stuffing your mouth with a nerf-type ball will also do nicely!

Remember, our first response is often to give advice or sage words of wisdom. Our prophetic words plus a buck will buy us a cup of coffee too!

What the person most often really needs is to be listened to.

*****

As a listener, when we begin speaking enough lines to fill a paragraph we have probably said too much already.

Who came to talk anyway?

*****

The best way to be that mirror for the speaker is to take what she said—the feelings, themes, central issues, concerns—and in one or two sentences *rephrase* them back. For example, Cindy

60

speaks for thirty minutes about the pain of broken and disrupted relationships in grade school, high school, and now in college.

A simple...

"It must have been really tough during these years," or "It must be hard to even think of becoming involved again," or "Good relationships seem to be difficult to come by for you," will suffice to show Cindy that you are hearing her, trying to understand her, and that you want her to continue. It's hardly rocket science, my friend.

*****

A good way to begin many of our responses would include:

"It seems as if..."

"It appears to me that..."

"It sounds as if..."

"What I seem to be hearing is..."

"I think I'm hearing you say that..."

"If I hear you right, you're saying that..."

"If I could sum up what I hear you saying..."

*****

Tentative, more gentle phrases are most helpful in responding to others. To say that "you *are* feeling this..." is often overly presumptive on the part of the listener and smacks of analysis.

A few words like "could it be that..." or "some of what I seem to be hearing is..." are usually more helpful and inviting.

Just keep it short, simple, and minus the "counselorese."

*****

Listening skills are as crucial to living as the "Three R's,"
yet how many have ever had a course, lecture, or
homework assignment in this area?

*****

Sharing at increasing levels of openness and intimacy erodes the layers of protection and safety. The walls of security and self-delusion begin to come down, brick by brick. Or in a moment of dynamic insight they may be swept away in clusters like fallen leaves in high winds. To relate on this highest of levels is to share one's very being—the essence of one's very self.

*****

It seems that many of us learn to settle for or are resigned to accepting a kind of mediocrity in our lives. It is not that we do not have regular and rather routine tasks to perform daily, but that we live in such a way that keeps us from the possibility of feeling and experiencing any inordinate degree of pain *or* pleasure.

In a sense, *we become comfortable with our comfortableness.*

A good listener can help to move us off center.

*****

Change may indeed be painful...

...But then again, so is *not changing.*

*****

How do you choose to take your pain? Do you use your energy to stay in the pain or channel it towards a healthier way of life?

*****

A good listener can show you things
that you never knew or dreamed you had.

*****

Another word for crisis could be growth. A knowledgeable listener can help you to use your crises, pain, and confusion as an impetus for growth and re-direction.

It is interesting to note that the Chinese symbol for crisis is *opportunity.*

*****

"As we learn to put our problem in its true perspective it begins to lose the place of dominance it once held in our thoughts and our lives," is the watchword and prayer of all Al Anon members. Al Anon is a support group for those affected by another's alcoholism or chemical dependency. What a terrific promise that we can hold in our hearts as we seek to view our life and our struggles with a more lucid pair of eyes!

Good listeners are often the impetus for new found vision and aid in our ability to see that this problem is not as big or as life-encompassing as we once thought. We no longer "eat, sleep with, and drink" the problem but have put enough perspective on it that we can move on with our lives.

*****

A moment of insight or *new sight* came to me at a retreat where I was speaking about listening and relationships. I was told beforehand to try and talk towards the right side of the room where a lovely and partially deaf young lady was sitting. She could hear very little but was excellent at reading lips.

I thought to myself how sorry I felt for her condition and then thirty minutes into my presentation began to realize how much she was teaching me. For she was one of the most interested, animated, caring, and intense listeners to whom I had ever spoken. Being deaf had forced her to really attend to another ever so closely as this was the only way she could understand the person's words and feelings.

In all the talks and presentations I have given to scores of audiences, Gina remains one of the best listeners I have ever encountered. For someone who could *hear* so little... she *listened* so much... because *she listened with her eyes and her heart.*

*****

Attitudes, like bad habits, grow strong and die hard!
Listening is one of the rare life forces which has the
power to actually soften or change an attitude.

*****

Another lesson was learned when, much to my delight, I discovered a television feature on the life of the person who wrote one of my all-time favorite songs—"What A Difference You've Made In My Life." The gifted writer and singer is a blind man named Ronnie Milsap. His courage, strength, caring, and sensitivity were dynamically portrayed as he spoke and interacted with audiences, friends, family, and the TV interviewers.

His ability to listen to these people as well as to himself was vividly portrayed and greatly admired. His connection with the audience and those around him was unmistakable. And, most amazingly, the chat he was having with this skilled interviewer began to shift. Ronnie appeared to be the more interested party as he asked questions, nodded his head, and smiled. I don't think the interviewer quite knew what hit him!

How does one listen as he so beautifully demonstrates when he cannot see the eyes, facial expressions, and gestures of another? You have to have eyes to really listen, don't you? The answer has come to me:

Because he listens with his *ears,* and more importantly...

...his *HEART*.

*****

Our lives are made up of a variety of hurts and losses, minor and significant. They range from the loss of a favorite watch that breaks to moving to a new neighborhood, from ending a relationship to dishonesty in a friendship, from not having the kind of mom or dad we needed while growing up to the death of a loved one. No longer in a constant mode of striving, the death of a dream, or coming to grips with what will never be all take their toll. Perhaps our most significant loss is when we are forced to see the truth about something in our life which up to this point we were unable or unwilling to acknowledge and accept.

All losses cause us varying degrees of suffering. Many in the helping professions feel that the ability or inability to recognize, work through, and accept these losses and their accompanying pain is one of the most significant factors contributing to the quality of our present and future life, health, and relationships.

Having the liberty to feel and express this hurt through the encouraging and therapeutic ears of another will help us to more effectively work through our pain. Present losses do not get entangled with and attached to old ones. We become free to move on with life and open ourselves to new experiences and relationships. We release the dreaded fear of not wanting to lose again or resist the urge to close down and not risk because it is too painful. We no longer paint our world with the broad brush of what we are always losing or what should have been but rather what we *now* have, may indeed *gain,* and what there might *yet be.*

*****

A listening ear can help quiet the storm of the raging pain within.

*****

Years ago I recall doing one of life's most unpleasant tasks—saying goodbye to a friend and colleague. I hate farewells. As I thought about her leaving and our relationship, like a lighthouse illuminating the darkened seas, it became clearer to me that she had become more than just a friend. She was a confidant and an unconditional listener. I could commiserate with her about my concerns and frustrations with teaching and students, share my inadequacies as an instructor, give voice to my crazy notions and dreams, and laugh with her in humorous irreverance about education and college life... and still know that I was okay.

Why hadn't I realized what a good friend she had become until the final days before her departure? My parting words sprang from this revelation: "You have been a terrific listener to me. I'm really going to miss you." I truly do appreciate and miss her. Good listeners and friends are not always easy to come by.

*****

A listener's trust implies that whatever is said here *stays here* and will never leave the place in which it was discussed. You have entrusted to me a very special part of who you are and to this I will pay the highest respect by keeping our conversation between the two of us.

*****

It was almost nineteen years ago that a nursing supervisor asked me to do a short workshop on active listening for the staff at our hospital. I worked several hours in preparing the presentation and came up with about twenty minutes worth of material. My notes covered one sheet of paper.

Since this time I have had the opportunity to present the topic of listening hundreds of times. My notes now span countless pages and can take up to a week to present. In fact, they turned into a book!

Did I do a lot of research in the area? No.

Did I read a bunch of books on this topic? No.

Did someone give me notes or information about listening? No.

You see, the more I had the chance to talk about the topic of listening, the more I learned about this skill. For as I expressed my thoughts and experiences, new ideas, insights, illustrations, and perspectives came (and continue to come) to my mind.

As people *listened* to me speak, I gained new understanding into this area of life.

This is exactly what we do as a listener—help the speaker expand and gain new perspectives.

*****

One of the best ways we can often help another is to listen to him with our "gut." What does this mean?

Simply stated, many times a person will be talking to us when we begin to get a kind of knowing or gnawing feeling in our stomach. It is a twinge of uncertainty in our mind or heart that what he is telling us is not completely accurate. We sense that he may be twisting something or even hiding a fact. It's as if what he is saying does not mesh with his actions, beliefs, or what he has told us previously.

Our gut often tells us that something may be amiss in what the speaker is expressing. When appropriate, it is important for us to check this out. We do not have to be analytical and give many specifics as to why we get this feeling. Merely point out or suggest to him that we are perceiving certain feelings or signals about what he is saying and then relate our observations.

It is true that some of our gut reactions may be inaccurate, distorted, or clouded by our own issues; however, if we know ourself well enough, they are often worth investigation.

66

Perhaps there is denial on his part. Let it lie there and then go back to it when the opportunity arises. The speaker could be becoming aware that you are on to him and that eventually he may think, "Here is a person I can talk to."

Even if your gut reaction is not accurate, you have let the speaker know you are trying to understand or, indeed, encouraging him to clarify what he is thinking and feeling.

*****

Another general helpful tip can be taken from the previous suggestion. If at *any* time you feel that you do not understand or accurately perceive what another is saying or that she may be speaking too quickly, take the time to stop, clarify, and check this out with her.

What a wonderful world this would be if more of us made the effort to insure that we are hearing another correctly and understand what is being communicated to us.

Can you imagine how much more pleasant family life, friendships, and the workplace would be if we did this? It's not hard, but it takes a little bit of time and work on our part to accomplish. There's that word "work" again.

How do we do it? A simple *"Back up for a minute, let me see if I got this,"* or *"I think I lost you, can you repeat what you just said?"* or *"Can you explain a bit more about what you are telling me?"*

A favorite of mine is to hold up my hand in the universal "T" shape and say *"time out!"* This is especially helpful when listening to kids.

*****

Our attentiveness as we listen is imperative when demonstrating that we care about the speaker. In fact, it is sometimes more important to look as if we are listening than to actually be listening! The speaker will soon realize whether or not you are listening by how well you attend to her.

Lest it sounds as if all we need to do is fake it and appear to be listening, it is not. Non-verbally giving messages or cues to the

67

speaker that you are sincerely interested is often the invitation they need to be more open.

The trick for us is to join genuine listening with the potent reinforcement of non-verbal attending. This combination can be incredibly powerful.

*****

In the classroom I never ceased to be amazed how often students would vociferously contend that they were interested in a topic or a speaker; however, as I observed them listening, they seemed anything but involved listeners. When confronted with their lack of apparent outward interest, many of my students were quite surprised and often defensive. Even though they were indeed listening to the speaker (haven't we all sworn we were listening to someone, albeit in a lackluster way?!), they had not yet developed the art of non-verbal listening.

Several students worked very hard at this aspect to the point of actually practicing some helpful gestures in the mirror. Here are a few of the techniques that we discovered aid in this process:

• Look the speaker in the eyes. One person suggested that if you had difficulty in maintaining eye contact, then look between her eyes just above the nose until you become comfortable!

• Face the person as directly and squarely as possible. Don't be turned sideways or at an angle.

• Put down what you are doing. Stop reading or listening to the radio or TV. People know when I am not in the mood for listening. I usually continue doing whatever I am doing, look up sparingly, leave the TV on, or refuse to put the newspaper down!

*****

Remember how much it meant to you when your mom or dad put down the newspaper, sewing, screwdriver, or book when you wanted to talk to them? It spoke volumes to you—much more than words. Here are a few more ways to say "I'm listening."

• Lean slightly forward towards the speaker. This seems to be

68

symbolically saying that "I'm interested and willing to be involved with what you are going to say." In the Good Book, Proverbs talks about "inclining" your ear towards the speaker.

• Nod your head, furrow your brow, widen your eyes, gesture with your hands if appropriate.

• Get on the person's physical level whenever possible. This is especially important with children. Stoop down, kneel, sit in a smaller chair, or whatever you must do to interact with them on an even level—at the same height—eye to eye.

• Be as open as possible in your posture. Rigid form, crossed arms and legs, etc. may often be the mark of an uninterested or uncomfortable listener. An open appearance may literally and symbolically demonstrate a willingness to listen and further encourage the speaker's openness. It says to another "I am open and receptive to what you have to say."

Obviously we can only be as relaxed as our own comfortableness allows or to the degree of intensity that the speaker's dilemma might dictate. For example, if you are ill at ease with the topic of divorce or alcoholism, then you cannot expect to be very relaxed when listening to someone talk to you about it.

In case you are wondering, yes, we covered this stuff in another part of the book. And no, I am not putting it in twice because I need to fill a certain amount of pages. It's because I hope you will get the point of just how *very important* I feel the listener's non verbal-skills are. Look out. I may even stick it in a third area of the book too!

*****

Closely related to attending skills are the brief verbal acknowledgments or, as I have so fondly heard them called, "*encouraging grunts!*" Some of them include:

"Hmm..."

"Uh Huh..."

"Ugh..."

"Ooh..."

"Whoa!"

"Oh..."

"Ah..."

"Woo..."

"Yikes!"

"EEEK!"

"Bummer!"

"Hmph!"

"Geez..."

"Yow!"

_____ (what's your favorite?!)

These grunts, combined with the appropriate non-verbal gestures, are a great reinforcer for further conversation, a sign that you acknowledge the speaker's feelings, and an invitation to keep going. It's highly technical, eh?

*****

A friend of mine who I consider to be a terrific counselor often does therapy with children. As we know, children often yell "ouch!" (as do adults for that matter) when they are in pain or have been hurt. So what did Dave frequently do when a young person talked of their emotional hurt or the pain of something going on at home? He gave a slight wince or grimace and his best empathic and emphatic *OUCH!*" How the kids responded!

*****

"Minimal prompts" are handy and simple ways to encourage a person to begin or continue talking. They're hardly graduate level stuff; but if expressed with *sincerity*, they are a wonderful way to encourage a sense of openness and caring. They also serve the vital function of helping to clarify what the speaker is saying. In very few words these prompts speak volumes about our attempts to connect.

Again, in tandem with appropriate non-verbal gestures, these can be powerful reinforcers. Here are a handful. You can add a few of your own to the repertoire!

"I see..."

"Go on..." or "Tell me more..."

"Keep going..." (throw in a circular hand movement)

"Whoa... back up a moment..."

"Time out" (or I often simply hold up the universal time out symbol - "T" shape made with both hands)

"I think I lost you. Let's back up..."

"And then...?"

"So you...?"

"In other words..."

"So I think I hear you saying..."

"Let me see if I got (heard) this right..."

"It seems as if..."

"It sounds to me like..."

"What I seem to be hearing you say is that..."

"If I've caught it right, what I am hearing you say is..."

"If I could summarize what I hear you saying..."

"Because..."

"Translated that means...?"

*****

Another helpful technique to use, especially with children, is allowing them to express their feelings through a particular body part or object.

I recall working with a ten-year-old boy and talking with him in the game room of the hospital. He had difficulty expressing his feelings and at this particular time began waving the pool cue menacingly at those around him. I asked him what his stick was saying. He replied with authority, "It's saying that I'm tired of people getting on me for things. Just leave me alone."

The next day I saw him at the nurses' station and he was tapping his fist into the palm of the other hand as he talked softly about a certain nurse. I asked him what his hand was saying. He replied, "It's saying that if that nurse gives me trouble one more time, I'd like to smack her!"

The active body parts and/or objects are often symbolic and/or expressive of what people are feeling and can often be a *safe* avenue for allowing them to talk about what is on their mind and heart.

*****

"If only I had," "I should have," and "I wish I never," are three of the saddest phrases with which we begin far too many of our sentences. Those who use such statements on a regular basis are under a constant strain and torment of thoughts and words that seem to eat away at their very being. While spending time on what could have, might have, or should have happened, they are using precious life energy to keep from moving on and experiencing their world. It's as if they are trading what might have been for what still could be.

It's great to have someone to talk to and help sort out many of life's possibilities.

*****

We can choose to experience the inevitable pain and hurt in our lives in two basic ways...

By deciding to defend, minimize, prolong, rationalize and stuff it away inside, or...

... by experiencing, owning, expressing, facing, understanding, and working to heal it.

Making any necessary changes is *your* call.

*****

A relationship which is full of sharing with, understanding of, and listening to one another does not just happen. Like a beautiful garden, it must be actively pursued, cultivated, and maintained.

*****

For a salesman to sell he must *listen well*. No matter what the business, providing services and products for another requires a good listener who can establish rapport, trust, and a sense of really hearing the needs and wants of his customer. The customer will feel valued and in turn the salesman will prosper.

*****

Listening without caring is *manipulation*.
Listening with caring is *Concern*.

*****

Some of life's most discouraging experiences are those that deal with parents who say "What happened? I had no idea this was going on."

Or, even more tragic are the words "If only I had listened to what they were trying to tell me."

Such are the stories which are repeated daily from a parent of a troubled or hurting son or daughter. *"If only"* are two of the most regretful words in our vocabulary. It's too bad the parents were unable to pick up on some of these things earlier with their kids. Just as regretful is that they did not have someone to talk to about what might be happening in their lives.

It's hard to see and feel what's going on when we are so close to the problem. The signs are tough to read when our eyes are closed or the blinders are in place.

*****

While conducting a workshop, I decided to give a three-minute description of a portion of my morning's routine. The group was asked to listen as intently as possible and then number and list each fact and incident as I had recited it. Next to each fact they were to imagine *every possible feeling* which I may have been experiencing. The total of the class's evaluation was eight specific facts and *thirty plus* possible feelings <u>behind</u> these details. Wow! (This is a *great* activity to do in small groups—any "story" will do.)

Ah, it's nice for a change to have someone center in on how I might be *feeling* instead of getting so caught up in the factual stuff. Far too many of us are graduates of the Joe Friday school of listening. Hey baby boomers, do you remember the show Dragnet?

"Just the facts ma'am. Just the facts."

73

We would do a lot more connecting with others if we took the approach of, "Not just the facts, Ma'am. We'd like to hear about the _feelings_ too!"

*****

The worst thing you can tell me at the moment I pour out an unexplored, suppressed, spontaneous, or previously unexpressed feeling is, "You shouldn't feel that way."

Don't tell me how I should feel or should not feel. Just give me the freedom to feel.

We can discuss all of its implications later, okay?

*****

Encouraging the speaker to say, "I feel..." as she begins many of her thoughts and sentences helps her to get closer to her feelings, fears, and desires. "I feel... angry, hurt, scared, or embarrassed" tells me who you are and helps you to more fully realize and own what you are experiencing.

Once identified and given a name, you can now begin to do something about a feeling or issue.

*****

A person who continually begins his sentences with "I think" probably spends an inordinate amount of time with and gets stuck in his thoughts. It is difficult to travel to our feeling world when we remain in the safety of our thoughts.

*****

When you tell me what you think,
I get to know your thoughts and ideas.
When you tell me what you _feel,_
I get to know _You._
Big difference.

*****

"I feel... (supply any feeling word)" and "I feel _that..._" look the same, but are worlds apart in their meaning.

"I feel that..." is another convenient way to keep from owning and describing how we truly feel. Take out the word "that," please

74

and plug in a feeling word. Easier said than done!

*****

A friend and colleague participated in a marriage workshop where the couples were asked to read from a list of one hundred "feeling words" (adjectives, adverbs, etc.), placing a check mark next to those they were aware of knowing and/or using. The wives averaged seventy words. The men averaged thirty five.

At another workshop on marriage a more vivid example demonstrated the difficulty many men have in understanding and expressing their feelings.

For a non-stop period from Friday evening until Sunday afternoon, the group was bombarded with written and oral assignments to reflect upon, listing and relating their specific feelings about a variety of topics. Most of these feelings related to the participants' needs and concerns as individuals and couples.

Much of the time at this seminar was spent in groups of four couples in which the participants shared these feelings with their mates as the group leader and others observed. Many of the men were very cerebral graduate students— knowledgeable and fluent in a variety of foreign languages. Feelings were their toughest foreign language though, more difficult to decipher and translate than the most ancient of Greek and Hebrew scriptures.

"I feel *good* about..." and "I feel *bad* about..." were the basic ways they described their feelings. The leader should have made a tape of these responses, they were used so much! Participants were continually encouraged to express how they were *specifically* feeling. The husband might become flushed, flustered, and stutter.

"I mean I feel... (long pause, eyes look skyward, face tightens, and deep breaths are taken).

"I feel goo..."

"I mean I feel happy, sad, frustrated..."

Great! A revelation indeed. And what smiles this brought to all of their faces and satisfaction to each of the couples. By Sunday afternoon they had to keep each man to three feelings for every topic (out of the 10-15 they had listed!) so that the group session would finish on time. Recent research seems to indicate that men are as sensitive as women and sometimes more so. Their struggle has less to do with feeling and more to do with expressing.

I hope you are still working at it, guys.

*****

Instead of reaching for another medication...
...Reach out for a listener.

*****

One of the most simple yet effective techniques for helping people to clarify and express more fully their thoughts and feelings is that of repeating back to them a key word or short phrase from their sentence.

The operative or key word may be one that causes the listener some confusion or uncertainty, that demonstrates lack of clarity about what is being felt or said, or seems to be at the heart of his issue. A few examples might help.

Speaker: "I feel really bad about last night."

Listener: "Bad?" or "Last Night?"

Speaker: "What a lousy situation to be in."

Listener: "Lousy?" or "Situation?" *or*

"Lousy situation?" or "To be in?"

Speaker: "I gave it my all."

Listener: "All?" or "My all?" or "Gave it my all?"

· You will be amazed at the responses elicited from this little technique. A small amount of practice on your part could pay great dividends in help for a friend or family member.

Now you try one.

Speaker: "I'm tired of how messed up my life is."

Listener: "_____" or "_____"

or "_____"

Possible answers: "Tired?" or "Messed up?" or

"How messed up your life is?"

*****

76

I spent a couple of hours in a fifth grade classroom as the expert counselor who would talk to the students and answer their questions about life. I was not prepared for the depth of their questions, issues, and thoughts. I was not ready for their intense level of interest, attention, and listening.

I was surprised to hear about their hurts, fears, and relationship struggles. I was taken back by their consideration of, care for, and openness to me in their verbal and written "thank yous."

I hope they ask me back. I learned so much from them. I did not realize that the struggles and pain at my advanced age were so similar to theirs at age 11.

Thanks, kids.

*****

Often a good listener is the person just...

... living next door

... a phone call away

... the next desk over

... weeding their garden

... cooking in the kitchen

... in the office down the hall

... three rows ahead in church

... singing next to you in the choir

... on the sofa reading the newspaper.

*****

There are still so many things that I do not know about myself. Risking, challenging, and talking will bring me closer to some of them. Another's ears will help in this process.

*****

Many of us take great pride in keeping up
with our bills, housework, and reports at work.
Staying current and in touch with our feelings
would be a good one to add near the top of this list.

*****

For some of us the anxiety of listening to, accessing, and expressing our feelings is greater than the fear of losing our own life or of having a loved one die.

*****

Empathy is not trying to feel just like another; for no one can do that. If you say you know exactly how I am feeling and thinking then that is my first clue that you really do not. My hurt is not totally like your hurt. My pain is not entirely like your pain. My joy is not a perfect likeness of your joy.

You do an injustice to me and I to you. Although our experiences and feelings may be similar, they are not the same. Each has its own history, flavor, intensity, and color.

We *honor* and respect our uniqueness by hearing and allowing for the differences in one another's feelings and thoughts. If you presume to know "just how I am feeling" you may indeed miss "just how I, indeed, *am* feeling!"

Don't miss that...

*****

In case you have not noticed, feelings do not come in goods or bads, rights or wrongs, shoulds and should nots. They are neither moral nor immoral but rather a vital force in our life to which we are compelled to listen and respond.

The wrongness or immorality of our feelings belongs more to how we deal with them rather than the actual feelings. It's not about *what* we are feeling as much as *how* we express and manage our emotions. To feel is to once again validate our humanity.

*****

Isn't it nice to have at least one person in our life to whom we feel no compulsion to have to defend or minimize our feelings, thoughts, and desires... nor to have to be rational with all the time? Now, that's a good friend!

*****

Admitting to and actually saying the word *Anger* (or *"I am Angry"*) is highly analogous to the difficulty we have saying the

78

words "He is *Dead*," "She's an *Alcoholic*," or even "*I Love You*." There are just some realities we do not want to face.

It is a real breakthrough when a person can move from saying "I'm a bit disappointed" or "I'm a little bugged by that" to "That makes me angry" or "I'm angry with you."

Truly owning our feelings to their full depth and extent can be the most vital step in resolving them. A good listener can help cut through the euphemisms to the truth of the situation—moving us closer to acceptance and letting go.

*****

Ambivalence is a fifty-cent word for saying "I'm torn up," "I can't decide," "I want to... but I don't want to," "I know it's for the best... but I'm scared," or "I love him... and I hate him."

It is something that stares us in the face, can immobilize, or arouse continual anxiety.

What a relief to express these opposing or conflicting feelings —to confirm that they are normal and then begin the sorting-out and working-through process.

*****

A counseling supervisor gave us some rather sage and technical advice one day. He said, "If you are not quite sure what the person is feeling, take a guess at it."

Take a guess at it?!

Yes, take a guess at it.

You know, he was right. If you are earnestly attempting to connect with and hear a person and are not quite sure of his possible feelings, then throw out some possibilities of what you think he may be experiencing. If he senses that you are sincerely attempting to understand, he will often do one of the following...

(1) Tell you he does not feel this way,

(2) Tell you he might feel this way,

(3) Tell you he feels parts of these feelings,

(4) Tell you he does feel this way,

(5) Tell you even more!

What you are doing for him is very important. For instance you may be:

(1) Demonstrating once again that you sincerely care and want to understand him,

(2) Putting him in closer touch with his feelings,

(3) Challenging him to clarify what he is feeling. ("No, I don't feel this way. I think it's more of _____..."),

(4) Causing him to deny that he is experiencing these feelings but drawing him closer to the edge of awareness,

(5) In a sense, letting him know that you are "on to him." Inside he may be feeling, "Hey, here's a person I could talk to about this when and if I am finally ready or need to talk."

Are we putting words in his mouth?

Not exactly, but we could be if we play the game of "you tell me your problem and I'll tell what you're experiencing, feeling, and need to work on." Sharing our reactions and ideas as to what he may be going through in a caring, almost tentative and soft spoken manner is a different story.

But what if you guess at a feeling or dynamic and after having heard his negative response, sense more strongly than ever that he really is actively denying it? In this case, you hopefully know the person and his degree of strength well enough to either challenge him again or back off. Give him some space and return to the issue when he seems more receptive.

Denial runs deep.

You are planting the seeds for future conversations and letting the person know that this is someone he could eventually talk to.

*****

When looking in a mirror, we can only see part of the picture —varying pieces of who we are. A person's reflection and perception may be affected by her mood and/or feelings about herself that day, the mirror's quality and shape, or the type of lighting in the room.

A compassionate, understanding, and wise listener can bring

the mirror's true image into much clearer focus for the one doing the looking (talking). We gain a greater glimpse of who we are.

*****

A good listener can help make a one-dimensional person...
...respond to life in a multi-dimensional way.

*****

On the surface, apathy manifests itself through a casual attitude, flat facial tone, and a blasé feeling for life. In reality, there is often a caldron of anger, hurt, or disappointment in one's self and others. Frustration, unhappiness, and disgust may lie just beneath the surface.

The best way I know to penetrate this non-caring facade is to begin transforming *apathy* by our *empathy*.

*****

Depression is experienced by every human being in varying degrees of intensity. It may range from a mild feeling of being down to a disorganizing debilitating state of being. Depression can be clinical and chronic or situational and episodic. It is almost as if our computer is jammed and we can no longer relate to our world. Even the most basic things—eating, sleeping, or just reading the newspaper—seem difficult at best.

What is often needed is a caring listener who can help begin to melt away the layers surrounding the buried feelings which are fueling this depression. Our depression is trying very hard to tell us that something is not quite right in our life and it's time to check it out.

For those whose depression seems to be recurring or intense, professional help is strongly recommended. Good listeners need to recognize when they are in over their heads with another's problem.

*****

Inevitably, every semester several students would turn in a project or report that varied slightly from the required format or in fact bore absolutely no resemblance to the directions given. And, just as the sun rises daily, so did these students vehemently argue that they followed the instructions and completed the work as requested.

It is at these precise times, that I would give anything for a videotaped copy of my original discussion and guidelines for these reports. Somehow just saying "This is how I told you to do it. How come most of the others did it correctly?" carried little meaning at this juncture.

Many have suggested that I give a detailed, printed description of how to do the project that would eliminate the unpleasant confusion and hurt which invariably occurred. It is a fine idea indeed; however, most of these students would be entering a profession in which they'd be (1) working under someone else, (2) paid daily to listen, and (3) constantly writing reports based on verbal instructions and communications. What a great opportunity to sharpen their listening skills!

Somehow they all did not see the value in what we were doing, especially when they received a "C" or were forced to repeat the assignment. I hope it helps someday.

*****

I was in the early stage of a conversation with a senior social work major and beginning to tell her something which was quite important to me. The previous semester this young lady had been in my class—a class, incidentally, with the primary emphasis on the importance of becoming better listeners.

As I began to tell her what was on my mind, she abruptly interrupted me to say, "I can't believe what we are covering in this other class. It's all on listening again like we learned in your class. I know that stuff already!"

Experiencing that sinking feeling of having been cut off and that what I had to say was not very important, the irony of having my student interrupt with this topic was not lost on me.

So you had this skill taught to you in one semester, got an "A," and you know all there is to it? We never do.

82

*****

Many of us go through our lives without ever seriously seeking to define, let alone "redefine" our values, goals, relationships, and the person we are becoming. What an exciting venture when we begin to challenge and investigate those beliefs about ourselves and our world that we have, up to this point, accepted carte blanche, no questions asked!

This produces a kind of dynamic tension that can be simultaneously frightening and exhilarating. It's as if we have awakened a new part of our being—the kind of feeling that gives us pause and exclaims, "Where did that come from? I never knew it was there!"

As we start to re-evaluate what it is we have become and chip away at those well-entrenched parts we need to let go of, we are put in touch with yet another dimension of who we are. Am I suggesting that we haphazardly disregard and reject all parts of our life which have shaped our being? Do we renounce those values and beliefs that have been instilled by our religion, parents, friends, and loved ones? *No!*

But can we give them more than a cursory glance and not simply pay lip service to the very forces that motivate our every movement? Don't we owe it to ourselves, our God, and our world to be in the continual process of defining *and* redefining our purpose, desires, and values?

*****

Before embarking upon an all-night spring break driving excursion to sunny Florida, I was to conduct my final workshop session at a tiny church in rural Ohio. Not being very familiar with the Buckeye State and having previously driven to this location each week with a colleague, I was fairly clueless as to where we were.

As I entered the church with atlas in hand, three men were there to warmly greet me. "Could one of you give me some idea of how I might best travel to Florida once I leave here tonight?" I asked.

No sooner had these words left my lips than one of the kind-hearted fellows began rattling off a detailed itinerary. In mid-sentence, another man grabbed the map out of my hand and set off upon a new set of directions. No sooner had he started talking when the third gentleman yanked the map out of his grasp and proclaimed, "No, no, no. I just got back last week from there. Here is what you want to do... !"

I never dreamed there were so many routes from this little town in Ohio! Each person seemed certain he had the best directions and, furthermore, could justify them with apparently sound and solid reasons.

Just for the heck of it, I tried taking one route down and an entirely different one on the return trip home. Alas, each was about five minutes and five miles within the other! Both had their strengths and weaknesses. Most importantly, I got where I needed to go.

The listening ear is much like a road map to us in that it provides for creative and alternate routes to our destination. Getting there is not nearly as important as the fact that we begin the journey and try the best route(s) available to us. In discussing our life's issues and problems, it is nice to know that we do have choices and alternatives.

There is often no *best* way.

Perhaps we just need to begin walking and talking with a listener. By the way, in light of how the men barged in upon one another with little regard to the other's ideas or feelings, I'd say we needed to extend the number of sessions!

What was the name of the workshop?

"Listen to Your Neighbor's Heart."

*****

The need to be listened to is perhaps one of the greatest unmet needs in many of our lives today.

*****

My good friend Dr. Paul Robinson adapted this helpful piece taken from the great psychologist Dr. Carl Rogers.

Can I Create a Helping (Listening) Relationship?

1. Can I be in some way which will be perceived by the speaker as trustworthy in some deep sense? Can I be dependably real or congruent? Can I be aware of whatever attitude or feeling that I am experiencing at the moment?

2. Can I communicate what I am experiencing, whatever feelings or attitudes that I am aware of, to the speaker (when such would be helpful)?

3. Can I let myself experience positive attitudes toward the speaker, or am I afraid to express warmth, caring, respect, etc.?

4. Can I experience myself as a separate person with separate feelings? Am I strong enough in my own separateness that I will not be downcast by his depression, frightened by his fear, engulfed by his dependency, destroyed by his anger, taken over by his desire for dependence, enslaved by his need for love? Can I enter into his experience without losing myself?

5. Am I secure enough within myself to permit the speaker her separateness? Or, do I feel that she should follow my advice, remain dependent on me, or mold herself after me?

6. Can I let myself enter fully into the world of the speaker's feelings and personal meanings without desiring to evaluate and judge him and with sufficient sensitivity so as to understand even those feelings and meanings that he only experiences as confusing or of which he is dimly aware?

7. Can I accept the other as she is? Can I relate this attitude? Or, do her words / feelings / actions threaten me and my sense of self?

8. Can I communicate in such a way that I free the speaker from the threat of evaluation or judgment?

9. Can I meet the speaker in a way that is confirming of his potentiality? Or will I relate to him as someone bad, immature, confused, neurotic, frightening, or crazy?

*****

85

Of all the risks we face daily, none can be so potentially devastating as the risk of feeling rejected. The risks involved are two-fold:

(1) Others will not like, respond to, or accept what we have to share with them,

(2) Our willingness to listen may be met by indifference, silence, resistance, and a verbal or non-verbal "I don't want to talk to you."

What will be your choice?

Will you choose to open up and risk feeling rejected, or will you refuse an opportunity to make contact and connect with another which in turn may become a life-enhancing act?

Unless we are open to risking rejection, we will never develop the kind of relationships and friendships that are built upon trust and true intimacy.

*****

It can be heartrending to witness the pain and agony each family member and close friend experiences when coping with a person with a chemical dependency or other serious problem.

Those affected—often out of love, embarrassment, learned helplessness, enabling, fear, false hope, or need to control—deny and cover up the problem as much as the person who has it. So critical for these people to realize is that like the chemically dependent person, they *also* need to talk about what is happening. They too are in need of help.

There are many listeners available but it seems that when something is literally staring us in the face, we are often the last to see, recognize, or discuss it.

A caring listener can help to open our eyes to the problem, move us toward the assistance we need, and guide us through some of the tough decisions that often lie ahead of us.

*****

A dilemma surfaces when we try to be a listener to another whose problem we are unable to see or perceive accurately. In the case of especially close friends and relationships, there are some things we *can not* nor *do not* want to see in them. It is at this time that a more objective, perhaps professional, listener is needed. The loving thing to do is to realize that you are not the listener who can best help here and, therefore, must entrust this situation to another.

*****

No matter how open, aware, and transparent we think ourselves to be, there is in each of us (as in the alcoholic and often his family and friends) some things that we just can not see, own, or recognize. It's like trying to read a book that is an inch from our eyes. Although it is so very near, it is impossible to decipher.

Indeed, often the closer we are to something, the more difficult it may be to see it. A problem can practically be screaming at us to be addressed, causing obvious problems, and be quite apparent to others. But no matter how loudly it calls our name, we cannot seem to hear it. And so it is with denial, the most popular of our defenses. As we learn to be better attuned to listening to ourselves as well as to others, breakthroughs can and will happen.

*****

Did you ever stop to think that each of us has our own "*isms*?" Isms are those things in our life that we use to medicate feelings, those issues in our life we just can't seem to resolve, those struggles that often *control* us instead of us controlling them. Food, work, perfectionism, smoking, etc. would be a few.

*****

It was not uncommon to have the question asked of me, "Well, now that I am more in touch with myself and my feelings, what do I do to get over the pain?"

"Trust the process."

"Trust the process?!"

Yes, *Trust the process*. Know that if you continue to put forth the effort to allow yourself to experience the feelings when they come up, express them when appropriate, cry over them when you need to, and generally accept them as a part of yourself, then the "process" will eventually bring about healing.

Oh, yes, there's one other minor detail: this process may involve some forgiveness on your part. "I could buy this 'process stuff' up until now," you say, "but don't start talking about forgiveness, okay? If you knew what they did to me you would understand that forgiveness is out of the question."

Well, my friend, the cycle of the healing process is often left incomplete without the dynamics of forgiveness being included.

Forgiveness may involve offering it to another, asking it from another, or, you guessed it, bestowing it upon yourself. The act of forgiving oneself is perhaps the most difficult—yet is crucial to growing and moving on. Forgiving ourself is what often determines if and how we will forgive others, for it seems that there is a direct relationship between the ability to forgive ourself and the forgiving of others.

*****

I never did very well in my Greek classes, but there are a few unforgettable things I learned. We came across a favorite scripture of mine which said, "Jesus wept." That was a popular verse because I used it whenever I needed to recite one at Sunday school or vacation Bible school. It was kinda easy to remember. It's now an important verse to me for another reason.

Translated from the Greek, the word "wept" in this context means a bitter outpouring of grief. When Jesus saw that His good friend Lazarus was dead and realized how much He and those who had loved him were hurting, He expressed an intense level of grief.

It is a wonderful model for our humanity. *It's okay to cry*. In fact, there is great healing in our tears. It's no coincidence that the tears we shed while slicing onions are different than those we release when we hurt. Tears of emotional pain contain cleansing and healing properties.

Another lesson relates to Matthew 18:21-22. Peter has been getting some rough treatment, so he asks Jesus how many times he must forgive this person. Jesus replies, *"Seven times seventy,"* to which Peter is greatly surprised.

As I read this dialogue I thought, "Hmm, I'll forgive someone seven times seventy which equals 490 times. But on the 491st time, look out!"

Isn't it interesting that the Greek word for "seven" is "infinity?" Healing the hurts and the act of forgiving are not usually one-time events. Rather they are action words and, as in the case of our grieving, denote a *continual* process. It's not usually a matter of forgive and forget, but rather *forgive and forgive.*

*****

I used to repeatedly hear from my students how effective they felt they had become as listeners or how interesting a particular class was. This might have been true but I still could not feel it when I saw them scribbling on the side of their notebooks, gazing out the windows, or looking like no one was home. There were times I wanted to say, "You could have fooled me!"

The non-verbal aspect of listening cannot be over emphasized!

*****

Listening to others helps to renew the hope within
and shine a ray of sunlight on the darkest of struggles.

*****

Here's the paradox of being a good listener.

The more we can get in touch with the reasons we do not listen and indeed *recognize* when we are *not listening,* the greater the chance that we will listen more effectively. All the training and techniques in the world will not help if we are unable to break through to our negative listening patterns.

Anyway, being a good listener is more about *choices* than it is about techniques.

Textbooks cannot teach about matters of the heart.

*****

Rev. Paul Lintern of the First English Lutheran Church in Mansfield, Ohio, graciously allowed me to include the following article he wrote. He says so much in so few words...

"Just Being There Can Be Enough"

"Don't just do something, stand there!"

The words are written on a chalkboard in the pastoral care office of a Columbus hospital as a reminder to the seminary students training there as chaplains. It describes the ministry of presence.

The funeral home is sparsely attended by people who knew the deceased, and those who stream by and wander around seem lost, not knowing what to do because their assumption is that they are supposed to do something. They utter an artificial phrase, study each flower arrangement, and comment on how nice the body looks. They feel useless because they are not doing anything; but far from useless, they are being there for the family, for the hurting, and being there is ministry of presence.

"I want to thank you for being there for me," the young man says to the startled teacher who doesn't particularly remember doing anything for this boy. He didn't do anything; he simply was something—a listening ear, an accepting smile, an encouraging presence—the ministry of presence.

In a world of accomplishments, where we are featured in the news only if we do something, especially if it is bad, the ministry of presence is nearly invisible, and yet it is the most profound thing one can do for another in times of grief, vulnerability, loss, sadness, fear, or emptiness.

The little girl does not need a lecture on growing up when frightened by the lightning; she needs someone with her, holding her, rocking her.

The man in the intensive care waiting room, worried about his wife, can't say it, but is eternally grateful that one of his friends is sitting up there with him.

For the group of people who get together each week for lunch at the church, food is secondary to the friendship and connection they feel from being together.

The patient in the hospital bed has had streams of hospital employees come in and "do" something to him; he is grateful for the one who comes and just "is" with him.

The ministry of presence claims that we are human "beings" first, and human "doings" second, and that the time of being there for someone is a profound divine time that transcends the human hand and reveals the heart of God.

It is a ministry everyone can do if they are willing not to busy themselves with doing something.

I must go now.

There is someplace I want to be.

*****

Today was a hard day for me. About three major issues in my life were pounding me from all sides and the word "hope" was nowhere to be found in my vocabulary. Those with whom I came in contact sensed something was wrong and a few dared to ask what was bothering me. But when I attempted to relate some of these concerns, I was met by any one of the following hurried replies:

"Things will look up for you."

"Don't be so down."

"This may be for the best."

"Cheer up."

"Don't let it bother you so much."

And even worse were those whose eyes left mine and followed the activities of another or started up a new conversation with a passerby. Couldn't they see how important these things were to me and how much I hurt? Why didn't they see my urgency to be heard and understood—to be cared about?

There must be someone who could and would be that person.

But who might I call? *And* could I handle one more person's inability to hear? That hurt almost as much as the original pain. I felt so rejected. It was a risk I had to take, for if there was ever anyone in need of a listener, it was this person, this evening.

Thank you, Susan, for being that person for me. Do you know that you went as long as twenty minutes at a time without saying a word, but *your eyes and your being with me said so much.*

The pain did not go away, but the edge was taken off. And do you know what? The next day enough energy had returned that it freed me up to clean the house, play some basketball, grade a few papers, work on this book, and watch a little TV!

***** \

To tell someone who is depressed to:

"Cheer up,"

"It'll get better," or

"Don't let it get you down" is on about the same level as...

...directing a blind man to see,

92

...encouraging a woman to wish away her cancer, or

...admonishing a drunk person to sober up immediately.

*****

Could it be that we have such difficulty listening to those people in our life who we regard as being beacons of strength and stability because we seek to draw these same qualities from them?

We tend to measure much of our own life in relationship to theirs. And if we would sense them to be struggling, hurting, or less than perfect, what are we afraid that might mean or say to us about our lives?

Hey, they are human too, and in need of our encouragement, support, and listening ear.

*****

Love often involves an *active decision* or *choice*.

And so it is with listening.

*****

Who listens to the listener...

...when the listener needs to be listened to?

*****

A once popular song goes, "Oz didn't give nothing to the Tin Man that the Tin Man didn't already have."

The power and prodding of the listening ear can help people to realize that they *have* what it takes to live life more fully. It can help tap into these resources that are lying dormant in the speaker's being.

*****

In the immortal Wizard of Oz, Dorothy pleads with the good witch to tell her how to get home.

Glinda replies, "Why, Dorothy, you've known all along how to get there."

And so it is often with our life. We have sensed or, in fact, have always known how to get home. What it took was a listener to help put us in touch with the answers, or to give us the encouragement we needed to find our way.

93

*****

After a talk I gave, a woman stopped to tell me a discovery she had made. "You know, Steve," she said. "I finally realized why I have not been able to hear God's voice."

Having struggled with this for years myself, I whispered to myself: "You tell me, we'll write a book, and then go on Oprah!

What was her answer?

"Because I never shut up long enough to listen!"

Wow. She's right! Listening to ourselves, another, and God are all intertwined. Learning to listen to one helps us to be better connected to the others.

*****

Alcohol, pills, chemicals, food, shopping, "busyness," sex, work, (you fill in your favorite), and a host of other items are excellent at anesthetizing our pain but they only deal with its symptoms. The next moment, hour, day, week, or year you can count on its certain return.

Talking and being listened to does more than mask the symptoms—it gets to the root cause and begins tackling the problem in a more permanent framework—from the *inside out*.

*****

Like a bridge over troubled water...
...so is a compassionate ear.
*****

Adults have better command of language than children and thus can use words to more adequately express how they are thinking and feeling. Young people often lack this capacity—especially children. They most often express themselves through their play. In fact, their play is their work.

How kids speak to those they interact with and treat the objects they play with can tell us a lot about their needs and feelings. It is important that we "listen" with an understanding and perceptive set of eyes to what our kids are trying to tell us through these areas of their lives.

94

Come to think of it, adults also do a lot of expressing through their behavior, actions, and play! They just seem to be a bit more refined, sophisticated, and subtle in doing so!

You can learn a lot just by watching.

*****

Oftentimes it is not simply what a person says but *how* they say it that counts.

Such things as tone and loudness of voice, spacing of words, voice inflection, and speech rate can tell you much more than the person's words. These are called "paralinguistic cues." It is listening *beyond* the words.

*****

One day I sensed one of my students named Lisa was angry with me. When the opportunity presented itself, I said, "Lisa, you seem ticked at me. Are you?"

"No," she said.

The *no* would have been more convincing if her voice had not raised an octave above normal or she had not said *no* so abruptly.

"Are you sure," I said.

"Well... I guess I am a little."

From there we had a great chat.

*****

Let me point out one caution when attempting to read a person's non-verbal or paralinguistic cues: Don't try to make something out of every motion and voice tone you perceive.

Listening to the non-verbal and paralinguistic cues should be placed in a healthy balance with the other aspects of listening we have been discussing. Reading too many articles or pop books on body language can turn us all into annoying and irritating amateur psychologists!

*****

The most important body parts we must learn to read
are the eyes—for the eyes have a difficult time
in disguising the true feelings of our heart.

95

It is not uncommon to ask someone, "How are you doing," to which they may smile (often quite weakly) and respond, "Just fine, thanks."

I would believe them except for the fact that their smile was missing something. It was a kind of "half smile" which never did reach their eyes. In fact, if you were to take a picture of the person and cut it in half (across the face and below their eyes) you would swear that you were looking at two different people. The mouth was smiling in order to give a certain impression but the eyes told the true story.

Good listeners look at the whole package.

*****

A friend of mine, Jack, is a fine counselor and skilled user of the "House, Tree, and Person" Projective Technique. In this interesting test, the participant is asked to draw a picture of either a house, a tree, or a person. Their artistic skill has little or no bearing on how the picture will be interpreted. Such details as *what* or *who* is drawn, darkness of the lines, placement of the various pictures on the paper, and other symbolic features are observed and interpreted.

It was uncanny how accurate Jack's perceptions were regarding what was going on in the life of the person who drew the pictures. It seemed that no matter how sketchy or poorly drawn the picture might be, he could pinpoint both general and specific problems that the person might be experiencing. Jack's opinion was that he cut his counseling time in half with those who took the test. They were able to get to their genuine issues and concerns much more quickly than by the more conventional methods of psychotherapy.

A favorite story that Jack relates is that of being stumped with a particular client's drawing. He took the picture to his dad who was one of the finest psychologists utilizing this test at this time. After briefly looking at the drawing he said, "Why Jack, the man appears to be an alcoholic."

96

This surprised Jack since he had never even had a hint that the fellow might have a drinking problem. At the next counseling session, Jack explored his client's drinking habits and, sure enough, there was sufficient evidence to indicate that he indeed did have a problem with alcohol.

How did Jack's dad know this? By picking up on several different aspects of his drawing, all indications pointed to a possible drinking or dependency problem.

Witchcraft, you say? Luck? Guesswork? Not really. As Jack is quick to point out, an often repeated verse found in Proverbs best sums up the basis for this test.

"What a man thinketh in his heart, so is he."

In other words, the concerns, fears, struggles, hopes, issues, and desires that dwell inside ("in your heart") can not help but be projected or played out in some way in our outward life ("so is he").

How we feel and think about ourselves—no matter how adept we are at concealing it—will, to some degree, manifest itself in such areas as the way we dress, write, act, draw, behave, play, work, and interact with others.

It's powerful stuff!

*****

It's probably fairly accurate to say that
behind every healthy woman...
...was a little girl who was listened to, and
behind every healthy man...
...was a little boy who was listened to.

*****

I had the opportunity one evening to hear a fine jazz ensemble perform in a little tucked-away night spot in Chicago. The people at our table were jazz buffs and, hence, listened with genuine interest to the group. They were generous with their applause and quite attentive to each of the group's members. Others in attendance seemed more intent on drinking and socializing with their friends.

On several occasions, the musicians made direct contact with us, often smiling and nodding their heads. After the show we went up to tell them how much we enjoyed their music and, to my surprise, the vocalist and piano player were quick to say, "Thanks so much for your interest and good listening. We noticed! It meant a lot."

Ah, the awesome power of the listening ear being demonstrated once again.

*****

It seems that one cannot walk down a street, ride a bike, or fly on a jet without continually coming into contact with someone listening to a personal stereo with headphones or a blaring box of shiny metal pumping out the latest in rap, rock, or top forty. What a convenient way it is to avoid the world. This seems so symbolic of how adept we have become at being oblivious to what is going on around us and what others are trying to say.

How do you continue to tune out the voice within as well as the voices without?

*****

A dilemma that we face regularly is attempting to make a decision that encompasses two or more of our values in life. For example, a student may equally value good grades and her social/personal relationships. What happens when she has a paper due on Monday and yet on Saturday has a great opportunity and need to be with some good friends? How or can she balance the two?

What do we do when two of our values or needs seem to conflict?

Talking it out is a good start.

*****

Every time I meet or talk with a person who is physically or mentally challenged in some way, I am reminded of my own "handicap" of closing my ears, maintaining some negative or self-defeating habits, and not always doing things in my own or another's best interests.

We all have our handicaps.

We are all *challenged* in some way.

*****

Listening to another is one of life's highest forms of praise.

*****

When will we finally come to terms with the fact that we are not okay for *what* we do but for *who* we are? It is not our ability to hit a baseball, sing a song, or paint a picture that makes us worthwhile but because we were created as a unique individual by a Maker who cares about each one of us.

Affirmation by an interested listener helps us to become more aware of our special qualities. It assures us that we are indeed worthwhile because of *who* we are and not merely *what we do*.

And as I've heard it said, when it comes to our work or career, making a living is *not* the same as making a life. Furthermore, if we are *what* we do, then *who* are we when we're not doing it?!?

*****

One of the most exciting moments in life is when we have the experience of waking up to a new or sleeping side of ourselves. We ask "Where did this come from?" or "I never knew I had these feelings and thoughts in me."

It can be both scary and exhilarating for we have accessed yet another aspect of our multifaceted selves. These discoveries come most often when sharing with another.

*****

A mistake we often make is assuming that one listener can and will meet all of our needs to be heard.

It's important to have several people with whom you can talk because just as there are no two people alike in this world, neither are there two listeners who are the same. In having a broad spectrum of people with whom to talk comes the opportunity to gain a variety of input and points of view, for each listener might

99

hear a different tone or paint a unique picture with your feelings. It's about perspective again, my friend.

Come to think of it, it is a mistake to think that only one person can meet all of our needs in most any area of life.

*****

Silence in a listening situation can be extremely therapeutic for the speaker. When no words are spoken for several seconds, the silence may seem like minutes or even hours to the listener.

The silence is interminable,

seems almost deafening and,

is most certainly, uncomfortable!

What may, in essence, be occurring are some very important things for the speaker including:

...re-experiencing a situation,

...getting closer to her feelings, or

...thinking through some of the solutions.

The silence may also represent the first opportunity in a long time (if ever) that she could sit back and reflect in an uninterrupted and relaxed manner upon her life. What a gift!

So why doesn't this kind of silence occur more often? Is it simply because silence is so uncomfortable that we break in with meaningless chatter and questions? It is precisely at this time (as in the case when we feel the need to give advice) that we should seek the nearest roll of duct tape and quickly, yet gently place a piece over our mouth!

Look down at the floor, hold a pencil, peer up towards the ceiling, gaze out of a window, or work on your breathing. Do anything to allow the person to sit in silence.

There is power in the silence.

It can be most therapeutic.

*****

The best counselors I know are not people who are experts in every counseling technique, theory, and skill but are the ones who first and foremost know, and are comfortable with, themselves.

100

There is a direct relationship between being in touch with oneself and in turn being in touch with what another is saying. The skills are important but are merely learned mechanical techniques if the one using them has no understanding of human behavior—*most notably his own.*

A person who does not attempt to become aware of and understand his own needs, feelings, strengths, weaknesses, and behaviors will find it impossible to help another do that very same thing when listening to him.

Personal growth is imperative.

*****

Physical, spiritual, and social growth is a must also.

Because it takes so much energy to listen effectively, we need to take good care of these other areas of our life. Healthy nutrition; proper rest; restorative sleep; periods of relaxation; quality and fun times with others; regular strength, stretching, and aerobic exercise; and frequent chats with our Creator markedly enhance our listening quotient.

What have you done for your body and soul lately?

*****

By now you have hopefully been getting at least one strong message. That is, *balance* is central to not only being a good listener but also making a happier, healthier life. But a problem occurs as you become more adept as a listener. The result of having more people open up to you and the satisfaction you will derive from becoming close and helpful to others may cause your life to become out of balance. Too much giving and too little getting exacts a price.

On the surface this may sound selfish when, indeed, the opposite is true. In listening too much, we soon reach our saturation point—a level at which we no longer effectively hear others. This was vividly portrayed to me while I was working two different counseling jobs. I would leave after a full day's work at the local alcoholism center and then in the evening conduct

101

therapy in private practice with four consecutive clients. Near the end of the third session and into the fourth, my listening capacity would hit rock bottom. It was so bad that occasionally I wanted to give the clients their money back.

I found a very interesting dynamic taking place. It seemed that the more saturated I became, the less listening I did and the more *advice* I gave to people. It proved once again that giving advice comes more naturally and hence more easily when one is tired and lacking the energy to truly work at hearing others. Thus, by not allowing ourselves to *over give* by reaching this saturation point and by encouraging ourselves to realistically *get* what we also need from others (socially, personally, etc.), we become a more effective listener.

A few suggestions in this area would be to:

• realize that you can not be all things to all people nor be everyone's listening ear

• become more aware of your own possible need to please, to continually quest for approval, and be a listener to most everyone you come in contact

• cultivate the art of saying "no" more often—especially when it is not feasible, or when you do not have the time to listen

• ask yourself if by constantly reaching out to others, you may be avoiding taking an honest look at your own life?"

*****

Four questions I frequently ask helping professionals (and teachers too!) to seriously ponder are:

1. Is what I am doing with or saying to my clients or students *in their best interests or mine*?

2. Who *needs* this more (the listening or counseling situation), me or the one coming for help?

3. Am I getting most of my social, relationship, and intimacy needs met at *home* (outside of my work) or at *work* (with the closeness to clients or students)?

4. Does the client's or student's problem hit *too close to home*

for me? Am I knowledgeable about his problem area and am I the best person to help him? Would it be in his *best interest* to refer him to someone else?

*****

Isn't it amazing that during the course of a half-hour TV show or a two-hour made-for-television movie, one or more serious problems can be exposed, explored, explained away, and resolved? It is almost as if we too expect our life's struggles to be dealt with in equally quick fashion.

We want answers. Now!

The reality of the situation is that problems take time to be worked through or accepted.

Listeners, please be patient. The process of helping with your ears may be tedious and slow moving. This is not some prime time drama we are watching being played out on TV.

It is real life.

*****

I drove a friend down to the service station where her car was being repaired. It was fascinating to watch three mechanics working together to diagnose and remedy the problem. They continually asked questions, made suggestions, and listened to one another as they repaired the car. With each comment, a solution seemed more imminent. Alone and without the input of one another, I don't know if the problem would have ever been discovered. Together, they were close to finding the answer.

Synergy—what a marvelous concept!

And so it is with each of us in our daily life.

The synergistic effect of sharing problems, suggestions, ideas, and feelings makes everything go so much smoother. It not only helps to lighten the load but it also serves to expand our vision and connect with others.

*****

Those Dreaded Verbatims

I anxiously awaited the grade and comments on my first paper. It was probably twice as long as anyone else's and even beautifully typed in blue ink! It was a sure-fire "A" if there ever was one.

Just out of college and into graduate school (hey, it beat working at the time!), I was enthusiastically entering the world of becoming a counselor and was quite proud of the first of what was to be twenty-six more of these nasty things called "verbatims."

Each of us was assigned a section of the psychiatric hospital to visit each week, spend an hour counseling with a patient, and then eventually write up word for word *exactly what* was said, *how* it was said, and any and all non-verbal communications we witnessed. (It's a good thing I did this when I was young because now I'm lucky if I can remember what I said five minutes ago!) In addition to this, we were to write a commentary and evaluation section at the end about what we felt we did well or what we could have changed during the session!

The verbatim was typed with a wide left-hand margin, allowing for our instructor's comments. The one I submitted was about ten pages long and included fifty minutes worth of dialogue—a real masterpiece indeed! "I'll show these guys in my class *and* the instructor how it's done! Won't they be impressed by my skills and wisdom in working with people?"

I nearly grabbed the corrected paper out of my instructor's hands and hurriedly tore past his many written comments to where the grade could be located. After all, isn't learning about grades and approval? Certainly mine would rank high in both areas.

The last page and the grade it contained stunned me. It was a √-- along with words to the effect of "you saved yourself an extra minus because it was so well typed." And *I* didn't even type it!

A √-- was the equivalent of a "D-."

That week my feelings ranged from harnessed rage to quiet

despair. More than once the thought crossed my mind that I had either encountered an inept instructor or, more painfully, was not cut out for this counseling stuff.

Forcing myself to read his comments and feedback was not easy. Particularly pointed was the line, "Steve, this looks more like a lawyer's cross examination than it does a counseling session."

What he said next summed up the heart of what I had resisted yet desperately needed to learn. "You need to spend more time getting to the feelings involved in and surrounding what people are telling you and not get so caught up in the facts or content. How might the fellow to whom you are listening be feeling?!?"

I fought this "feeling thing" for the next two years of school. If you are carrying around a mind-set and attitude like I was, one that dictates that you see things in a fairly one-dimensional way, then listening with (1) judgment, (2) giving pat answers, and (3) no room for feelings is the only way to go.

Counseling was about giving advice, confronting, and fixing what was broken in people's lives anyway, wasn't it?

It was also much easier and more convenient to believe that we had a bunch of instructors who preached psychobabble and humanistic "mumbo jumbo" than to dare consider the importance of a trivial notion like feelings. I was not prepared for the gradual and often uncomfortable lessons I was beginning to learn: that the ability I had to shut down and out my own feelings dampened the receptiveness to hearing another's.

I am thankful that there were people who supported and helped me stick out this process. In reviewing my verbatims, I got better at reading the instructor's comments without just fast forwarding to the grade. After all, if someone was looking for a good counselor, would they be more concerned about that person's grade in Counseling 101 or their competency?

On a positive note, allow me to briefly revisit the final weeks of my counseling program. Same instructor. Same verbatim assignment (#25 I think). I turned to the last page for my grade and closing comments. They read, "Steve, it gives me great satisfaction as your instructor to see the progress you've made from your earlier verbatims. You are really getting it. Your ability to listen to others and their feelings has significantly improved. Your level of competence has risen tremendously." √++

After two (very often) long years of this message, it was finally sinking in. Some of us have a more rigid and entrenched viewpoint we need to lighten up on, or a more hardened heart we need to soften. I sincerely hope that for most of you this task will neither be as arduous or painful as mine. The fact that you are reading this little book and open to some of its ideas is a promising sign and a good start!

Remember, if you are willing to work at being at home with and accepting of your own feelings, doing it for another becomes more comfortable and natural. It's pretty simple stuff...

*****

Can you handle a couple of more verbatim stories?

Tom was one of the more advanced students in our group, having already been a counselor for a number of years. He was a person whom we all admired and with whom we all connected. He was friendly, fun, wise, and a caring listener to many of us young and very raw recruits.

Each week our instructor selected a different student's verbatim to review and critique. This session was to be Tom's. After giving a brief background of the client, we would proceed to review, read, and comment on the verbatim.

Before we began, however, our instructor posed a rather intriguing question. He said, "Tom, have you experienced a death in your own family or of someone close to you in about the past six months to a year?"

Looking rather startled, as if our instructor was some kind of mystic, Tom responded, "Ah, why yes, I have. A very special and close uncle of mine died a few months ago. He was kinda like a second dad to me."

Before Tom could say much more or ask him how he knew, our instructor said, "Okay, let's start reading this. How about if I be the client and you just go ahead and read your part, okay, Tom?"

As we moved through this verbatim, it simply reinforced what an excellent counselor Tom was. He was establishing rapport and building the framework for a relationship with this man. Somewhere in the middle, Tom asked him, "So what would you say are the biggest things in your life that brought you to the hospital for some help?"

"Well, my wife of thirty-five years died about seven months ago, and I just can't seem to get through it," he said.

"I'm sorry to hear that. It must be awful tough to lose your wife," Tom replied. "What other concerns do you have?"

The fellow went on to describe some other problems he was having, but they paled in comparison to the deep hurt over the loss of his wife. At this point, our instructor stopped the review process and looked at Tom. No words were needed. It jumped out at Tom as it did the rest of us.

It happens to even the best and most conscientious of listeners. Instead of pursuing the obvious issue of death and grief which was screaming to be heard, the subject was avoided because it hit much too close to home. Rather than encouraging the man to continue his expression of hurt, thus rekindling Tom's own pain, he switched to something more emotionally distant and safe. It was a logical choice. It's called being human...

*****

You will certainly remember your high school speech class if you had the kind of teacher who took almost fiendish delight in never having an order to or schedule for each student's speech. She would simply look around the room for what seemed like an interminable amount of time, watching scores of frightened eyes nervously attempt to avoid making contact with hers. For two weeks you rehearsed and ruminated upon the speech, wondering

107

when your number would be called... kind of like your execution. "Ah, Mr. Powers, I think we will start with you today." Gulp...

This was roughly the same feeling we had during our verbatim seminar. No one knew when his verbatim would be picked, so we came to dread the beginning of each session. Having your verbatim poured over, scrutinized, and critiqued by nine fellow students and an instructor was a humbling experience. "Would I embarrass myself or appear inadequate?" were not uncommon thoughts. Or worse yet, "What if I really *am* inadequate or incompetent?"

With only two weeks left and two of us yet to be selected, it did not take a math wizard to figure the odds. Perhaps I could feign illness or have an out-of-town emergency suddenly surface. Actually, even two weeks in the hospital—any hospital—sounded inviting!

Week #9 was upon us. I was actually feeling up to the task, for I had turned in a pretty darn good verbatim that week. So if my number was called, I was ready.

"Hi everyone," our instructor Ron said. "Today we will be taking a look at Steve's verbatim. Why don't you go ahead and tell us a bit about your client's history and reason for coming for help."

That out of the way, Ron said, "I think we'll do something a little different today."

"Oh great," I thought. "It's my turn and Ron decides to change our comfortable routine and be creative."

"Steve, I'd like you to be your client and read his lines and the rest of us will read your words and be you. And, how about if you sit over here (motions to a chair located off by itself) and the rest of us will sit in a kind of semicircle around you."

"A bit odd," I thought. "But what the heck. He usually seems to know what we need to help us become better listeners and counselors."

The process began, and after a few awkward moments, I felt

108

pretty comfortable. As it progressed we, in essence, put the written verbatim aside and immersed ourselves in the given roles. One by one the questions were asked and comments made by my fellow students facing me.

Before long, some of them even spoke on top of the other's words to get their points and queries across. It seemed like buckshot from a rifle: first this person, then that person, and yet another one over there.

Look out! Duck!!

I discovered a tide of anger and frustration mounting within me as their once thoughtful and helpful questions seemed more like an invasion. This once caring circle of colleagues and counselors felt more like a faceless firing squad.

With chest pounding, fists clenched, and a flush on my face I screamed, "Shut up! Just all of you shut up. Please!"

"Yo. Where did that come from?" I thought.

Ron looked at me and said, "How do you think your client felt when all he kept getting from you was rapid fire questions—from here to there, right field to left field—with virtually no time or permission to think *or* feel?"

Ron, I hate your creative ideas but I am so fortunate to have had a mentor like you. Did I ever learn a most valuable lesson that day! Relax. Calm yourself. Use questions thoughtfully, yet sparingly. Remember what's important here. You're building a relationship, not a legal case.

Listen to the person, Steve.

Really hear him...

*****

I once had the opportunity to help coach a women's softball team. While hitting balls for infield practice I somehow caught my index fingernail and partially tore it off. Do you suppose I stood there and muttered, "Oh, I ripped my fingernail. It hurts a little."

No! Church league or not, I blurted out a few choice words as an expression of the agony I was feeling. When I initially hurt myself, a player who was a nurse cleaned and wrapped it.

Later that evening, I had my own game. Due to the position I played, even greater pain was inflicted on my finger. Playing first base caused me to take a lot of hard thrown balls, so I placed a few pieces of gauze inside my glove to help cushion the impact. I must have presented quite a sight, for each time I caught the ball I was sure to tag the bag and then immediately jumped about a foot off the ground, letting out a muffled yelp from the pain.

"Boy is that guy an enthusiastic player. He gets excited just about every play," a few spectators remarked. It was as if someone was pounding my finger with a sledge hammer.

During the week the pain remained intense, so I took some medical advice from a doctor friend of mine. He told me how to best take care of it and I followed his suggestions faithfully. My finger continued to hurt over the next two weeks, and then into the third week something very interesting took place. After the third and final out of one of our games and after all of the post game rhetoric, a sudden and peaceful thought enveloped me. "It didn't hurt anymore. The pain was just about completely gone. The doctor was right. If you follow these suggestions, the wound will heal more quickly and completely."

A better analogy could not be made for our emotional hurt and pain. In time, with courage, and willingness to do the things necessary for dealing with a struggle, the wound will begin to heal. Some may take longer than others, for they cut more deeply and hurt more intensely. But they will begin to get better; and, hopefully, one day soon you will be ready to move on.

*****

"PEOPLE"

People. People [and listeners] important to you, people unimportant to you—cross your life, touch it with love and carelessness, and move on.

There are people who leave you and you breathe a sigh of relief and wonder why you ever came in contact with them. There are people who leave you and you breathe a sigh of remorse and wonder why they had to leave such a gaping hole.

Children leave parents. Friends leave friends. Acquaintances move on. People change homes. People grow apart. Strangers pass and move on.

Friends love and move on.

You think of the many who have moved into your hazy memory. You look on those present and wonder.

I believe in God's master plan in lives. He moves people in and out of each other's lives and each leaves his mark on the other.

You find you are made of bits and pieces of all who have ever touched your life, and you are more because of it, and you would be less if they had not touched you.

Pray to God that you accept the bits and pieces in humility and wonder, and never question, and never forget.

Author Unknown

Why is it that when we lose someone or something important to us we often do not fully realize it until they are gone? And to compound this pain, what a shame it is that we frequently use up much of our energy attempting to deny that we hurt or acting as if things were still the same.

A caring listener recognizes the hidden and suppressed hurt and encourages the person to talk about it as much as possible. It's not usually the speaker's anxiety, fear, and uncomfortableness with death, hurt, or loss which keeps him from broaching these painful topics. It's the *listener's*!

Many individuals who have experienced grieving relate that the most helpful people in their lives were those who had the courage to bring up the dead person's name and talk about their life. This in turn encouraged the bereaved to talk freely about the loss. Unfortunately, there are not many people willing to do that.

Keep in mind that no matter what the person may be showing outwardly, on the inside there is often a desperate need to talk— especially about the loss *and* life of their loved one.

*****

Listeners who are not afraid to discuss the feelings surrounding death or other losses are also needed with those contemplating suicide. Suicidal persons are most often helped by those who risk asking them any one of the following questions and then listening carefully to their replies:

(1) *Are you thinking about hurting or killing yourself*
or others?

(2) *Do you have a plan?*

(3) *What are the specifics of your plan?*

Many people who are successful in committing suicide often give some type of sign or message beforehand. And in general, the more specific and developed the plan, the greater the chance of carrying through with it.

Again, we are often afraid to bring up this topic when, in actuality, the person wants or needs to discuss it. Also remember that in the case of someone who may be suicidal, there is no such thing as confidentiality. You must tell people close to that person and enlist the assistance of helping professionals.

*****

When listening to someone who is anxious or fearful, it may be helpful to eventually weave into your discussion the following questions:

- *What are you afraid of losing?*
- *Is this fear a realistic or unrealistic one?*
- *Can you describe the possible consequences of what could possibly happen?*

Often the real issue involved is the anticipated loss of self-esteem if the person was to fail in some way. The fear of not being successful or of being thought less of by another often contributes to a fear that can immobilize us.

*****

Anger is perhaps the most misunderstood and disruptive emotion of all. It has been described as an *umbrella* feeling because it combines a variety of other feelings. Often it serves to mask underlying emotions such as *hurt, loneliness, fear, guilt, inadequacy, jealousy,* and *anxiety*.

When we feel hurt, we quite often become angry. When we are angry, we are usually hurt. In fact, anger is a natural progression and manifestation of our hurt. Simple, you say? Yes, except for the fact that many of us either do not know when we are angry or find it difficult to *own* and express it. How do we get it out and tell others?

Nothing excited me more in a counseling session than when the clients would say something like, "Now I see what is going on here. I'm *angry* at him."

Even though the anger may have been written all over their face, it can often take a long time for them to arrive at this awareness. Some of this expression of anger might even be accompanied by a variety of avoidance clichés such as "I'm a little

113

disappointed in him" or "It bothers me a bit that..."

The key, though, was that they were finally coming to terms with their true feelings—*on their own*. These are very human and normal feelings, and might I add, crucial to growth!

*****

When I hear someone say "I never get angry," alarms go off inside me.

"Don't you ever get hurt?," "Where did your anger go?," "What other forms is your anger taking? Sarcasm? Illness? Aggression? Stomach problems? Stiff neck or tight shoulders? Skin disorders? Headaches or back pain? Depression? 'Busyness?' Overeating?"

Consider the case of Jeff who was referred to me by the assistant dean of students because he had vandalized some dorm property while intoxicated. Jeff was a large and very skilled football player—a kind of "gentle giant" when sober, often speaking so softly you could barely hear him or giving a shy smile to those he passed by.

I asked him how he dealt with the times people hurt his feelings or when he became angry. He gave me a slight shrug of the shoulders and replied, "I learned that you just need to let things roll off your back. It's no use letting it bother you or getting angry."

Sure, it just rolls off his back and returns to his gut—with interest. "Jeff, can you see how the alcohol gives you permission to release the storehouse of anger being bottled up inside?"

Being angry is not wrong or sinful. The difficulty comes in being able to appropriately deal with it and express it. Playing a sport or engaging in a physical activity may reduce some of its intensity but the anger remains.

If you do not agree with me, think back to the times you were angry at someone and told yourself that it was not worth expressing or dealing with and that you were no longer mad at her. What happened the next time you saw this person (if you didn't go out of your way to avoid her)? You probably could not look her in the eye the way you used to, could you? The anger did not just miraculously vaporize and disappear.

You needed to talk to her.

Listeners, gently and with care, help that person to make contact with her hurt and anger and explore more appropriate and healthy ways to be free of it. Left unattended, these feelings will accumulate and continue to infect and affect our lives, just like any of the other feelings we keep inside.

*****

We often become victims of the "shoulds" in our life, allowing them to dictate how we live and how we feel about ourselves. Granted, some of these shoulds serve as healthy controls and moral guidelines. Other shoulds we could do without.

If I were to jump from a fourth-floor-window, there would be a price to pay. If we wrong another or are dishonest with him, there is also a price to pay. We live in a world designed for balance, homeostasis, and a type of cause and effect. When we do something contrary to good physical, emotional, and spiritual health we often pay a price. These shoulds are necessary to our well-being and enhance the quality of our relationships and life.

The shoulds we need help with are those that are neurotically fed or encouraged in us by a need to please everyone, to be a good girl or boy, or those that we constantly have had whispered to us by a past or present voice.

Try counting how many times you say the word "should" in an hour, a day, or a week. It may amaze you! Are these shoulds really in your (or other's) best interests or are they a kind of ritualistic and unrealistic need or drive you are bowing to?

Talking them out with an effective and compassionate listener helps you to break loose from these shackles.

*****

Much of our depression is rooted not only in some possible buried anger, hurt, or guilt but also in the numerous and often unrealistic expectations we place on ourselves. It is one thing to set workable goals and have hopes for which to strive. It is quite another to pursue expectations that are so high or unreachable that failure is the most likely outcome.

There is a fine line indeed between what is reasonable and may push us to become our higher, more productive self and what is so unachievable and unrealistic that we continue to perpetuate a kind of defeatist attitude about our life. The troubling part is that we continue to ride this merry-go-round in a cycle of expecting and demanding more of life than it can possibly give.

A finely tuned listener can help us to hop off the horse!

*****

One of the most liberating forces in life is freeing ourselves of some of the emotional baggage of the past. Much of this stuff continues to modify, motivate, and shape present feelings, attitudes, behavior, and relationships.

We do not look at the past to blame or avoid responsibility for our present situation but to gain understanding into some of the "whys?" of our life. Perfect parents, friends, and teachers have yet to be invented and until they are we will continue to feel their influences. After all, they suffer from the same things we all do— "terminal humanness!" As I recently heard someone so humorously say, "We are all products of a sexually transmitted disease called being human."

And this, of course, means we are all "C O Somethings" too. Children of _____ (you fill in the blank).

A good listener can help us to sort out some of this "stuff" including the values, desires, hopes, and expectations we wish to keep and those we would like to re-evaluate and possibly discard.

This same listener can also help us to work through more completely some of the lingering and possibly potent pain from a past experience.

Liberating indeed!

*****

Individuals and their pain usually contain at least one certainty. If they are in pain today and can not find someone with whom to talk, the pain will most likely still be there the next day. Often because of our need to help these people through their pain, we sometimes feel that we must be at a person's beck and call whenever they express a desire to talk.

Please hear what I mean when I say:

There may surely be times when we drop whatever we are doing, stay up into the late hours of the evening, or cancel some plans to be there for another. But we must also be realistic about how often and when we can be available.

The bottom line is this: Because we do care about our fellow human beings' struggles, we may be doing them and ourselves a greater service by waiting to listen to them when we have the time, patience, and energy. Their pain will still be there

*****

Always being willing to listen to someone at any time, any place, and in any situation can not only make for poor listening habits but will often lead to a great deal of anger—both at one's self (for not being able to say "no," having no time for yourself, etc.) and at the person who wants to talk (feeling that they are insensitive to your needs, too demanding, etc.). Unless you feel that the person is in some physical danger of hurting himself or another, you can usually wait for a more appropriate time to talk.

I finally realized that the best thing to do if someone called me at home after a long day or grabbed me as I was eating lunch or about to leave would be to get a brief idea of what they wanted to discuss, communicate my concern, and set up a time to talk. Interestingly, those who really did want to talk came back at our arranged time, complete with their pain, and often willing to work on what was bothering them.

Yes, some who did not come back took it personally that I could not see them right away. In most situations though, it was a case of their not wanting to work on their problems in the first place.

*****

117

ATTENTION
ATTENTION
ATTENTION
ATTENTION
ATTENTION
ATTENTION
ATTENTION
ATTENTION

ATTENTION

ATTENTION

ATTENTION

Now that I have your attention, I wanted to let
you in on the secret of all secrets to
becoming the most expert and
compassionate of listeners:

*(The more you begin to acknowledge that you are not truly
listening, the more likely you may then begin to genuinely hear.)*

If you feel that what others are telling you hits too close to home or triggers too many of your own issues, or that their problem is too serious and complicated for you to be of help, then please *know enough to refer them to a professional.*

Do not feel inadequate that you can not help them with this particular problem.

Do let them know that because you care about them they need to talk with someone who has greater expertise in their problem area.

Do help make the transition to this professional by possibly setting up the appointment or even taking them to the first session. This might be particularly helpful with such serious concerns as chemical dependency, abuse, eating disorders, grief, marriage problems, etc. because people dealing with these issues often need greater support and more direct intervention.

Do take the time to follow up at a later date, see how they are doing, and show your support.

Do realize that at first your friend may see this referral as a message that you are not concerned or interested. In time most friends will see the opposite—that you cared enough to help them in this way. In fact, don't be surprised if one day you receive a big "thank you" followed by the words:

"You know, you were the first person in my life who really called me on my behavior and problem. And what's more, you didn't just give me a bunch of dime-store advice. You made me do something about it! I finally got the help I really needed."

*****

Here's a word of *Caution:*

Watch for the all-too-common occurrence of:

"*I gave at the office and now I can not give at home.*"

Expending too much of our energy with colleagues, customers, or clients may render our listening tank empty when it comes time to listen to good friends and family members.

*****

119

I call Carl Rogers the "Father of Listening" because he, more than any other therapist, demonstrated the tremendous power of the listening ear.

From his classic work "*Person to Person: The Problem of Being*" consider the following words of wisdom regarding empathy. This is the true spirit and essence of listening.

"To sense the client's [speaker's] inner world of private personal meanings as if it were your own, but without ever losing the 'as if' quality, this is empathy, and this seems essential to a growth-promoting relationship.

"To sense his confusion or his timidity or his anger or his feeling of being treated unfairly as if it were your own, yet without your own uncertainty or fear or anger or suspicion getting bound up in it, this is the condition I am endeavoring to describe...

"It is this kind of highly sensitive empathy which seems important in making it possible for a person to get close to himself and to learn, to change and develop...

"I suspect that each of us has discovered that this kind of understanding is extremely rare. We neither receive it nor offer it with any great frequency. Instead we offer another type of understanding which is very different, such as 'I understand what is wrong with you' or 'I

understand what makes you act that way.' These are the types of understanding which we usually offer and receive —an evaluative understanding from the outside.

"It is not surprising that we shy away from true understanding. If I am truly open to the way life is experienced by another person—if I can take his world into mine—then I run the risk of seeing life in his way, of being changed myself, and we all resist change.

"So we tend to view this other person's world only in our terms, not in his. We analyze and evaluate it. We do not understand it.

"But when someone understands how it feels and seems to be me, without wanting to analyze me or judge me, then I can blossom and grow in that climate. I am sure I am not alone in that feeling. . .

"None of us steadily achieves such a complete empathy as I have been trying to describe, any more than we achieve complete congruence, but there is no doubt that individuals can develop along this line."

*****

Maintaining a confidence, keeping a secret, and being entrusted with another's feelings calls for a great deal of maturity by the listener. Our temptation to break this confidence often derives from our desire for approval and the notion we have something we think others want to hear. Some of us have even done it to hurt another.

A mature and caring person guards the entrusted words of another with honor and vigilance. They are sacred.

*****

A fine piano player approached me at a retreat and said, "Do you know what the sounding board does in a piano?"

Fumbling to remember my one year of childhood piano lessons, I said, "I think it helps the sound."

"Something like that," she said. "The sounding board directly affects the quality of the music and how well we hear it. It's a lot like what you've been talking about this weekend when it comes to listening."

Yes. Our listening to others serves as a kind of sounding board which resonates and reflects their feelings and in turn helps them to tune into themselves more fully and clearly.

*****

Bells should be ringing, alarms sounding, whistles blowing, and red flags flapping when a good listener hears someone utter sentiments such as "I feel *good*" or "I feel *bad*" or "I feel *stressed*."

The words *"good"* and *"bad"* are not feelings and fail to express the actual emotions being experienced. And "stress," our generations' catch-all phrase, provides few clues to what is truly going on.

Ask the speaker to keep talking about the situation and help her to be more specific. As she begins to name the feelings and clarify the real issues, discovery and new direction will happen!

*****

Gifted athletes, effective speakers, and successful performers all share one thing in common. Although they must follow specific plays, lines, or assignments, their greatest attributes lie in the ability to assess a particular situation and then intuitively know how to best proceed or respond.

Rather than spend valuable split seconds in thinking about what to do next, they are able to quickly read the proper signs and signals and instinctively react. This is the hallmark of all good athletes, artists, and performers. They progress from thinking to being, and doing.

And so it is with developing expert listeners. They begin to know how to effectively read the signs and signals given off by the speaker and are able to react and respond in a helpful manner. Having worked diligently at this art, they no longer need a great deal of time to think through everything that is expressed—both verbally and non-verbally.

They don't worry about having to say just the right thing or interact in the perfect way. Their more *intuitive* and accurate responses make for greater sharing and more intimate contact with the speaker.

*****

If by now you have gotten the idea that I do not like the word "advice," you are correct. Advice is one thing: considering alternatives and suggestions is quite another. Nudging, prodding, encouraging, and challenging are ways which I prefer to view this.

As a relationship deepens, the listener moves to an excellent position to assist the person in brainstorming and exploring practical, creative ways he may begin to deal with his situation.

This might include a verbal or written inventory of those aspects and forces which both positively and negatively affect the situation. Oftentimes the person with a problem is unsure of which direction to move. Now, with the listener, he can list and think through a variety of ideas. At this juncture it is important to be imaginative and willing to present as many options as possible, no matter how improbable they may seem, review these suggestions, and attempt to evaluate the best route to follow.

Once a plan is chosen, thoughtful attention should be given to *specific* and *measurable* ways in which the person may begin to carry it out.

*****

A helpful listener is one who assists another in making the best possible choice of which path to take at this time in her life.

*****

There are precious few certainties in this life, but along with death and taxes must come another, weeds! In what seemed to be an endless and fruitless task, I was pulling weeds the other day in my driveway. Nestled between the thousands of stones sprouted varying sizes and types of weeds. I methodically walked up and down the driveway slowly examining each section for the little green monsters.

Much to my continual surprise and dismay, I inevitably stumbled upon a group of new weeds. Just when I had been over that section for the third time or thought I was finally finished, there were more of the little buggers.

"Where did they come from?" I blurted out loud. I was convinced that they had popped out of the ground in the past five minutes.

Had I simply missed them the first two times?

Were they hidden behind some stones that might have been rearranged as I kicked and poked at them?

Did I not look intently enough on my initial exploration? Or was it because I did not really want to find them?

It sounds a lot like our life, doesn't it?

*****

From the little boy who yearns to be picked for the team to the woman who wants so much to be respected by her co-workers, we all need to feel that sense of acceptance by someone or some group. Nothing elicits this feeling of belonging more than the ears and heart of a caring listener.

*****

124

One Thin Dime

The lights were still on in the house as I entered the front door—late...really late. Much to my surprise and eventually my chagrin, there stood my diminutive mother appearing in less than the best of moods.

With one hand on her hip and the other holding what appeared to be a coin (odd I thought), she clearly and succinctly asked, "Do you know what I am holding in my hand? And furthermore, Steve, do you know what you can buy with it?"

It struck me as rather strange to be playing "Twenty Questions" with my mom at 12:30 in the morning. Figuring she would appreciate a quick and enlightened response, I fired back, "It's a dime and I could make a phone call." Correcto on both accounts. My lucky night. What do I win, Mom?

Well, your hunch about what happened is probably right on. Yes, I was two hours late. And no, I didn't call my mom to tell her. Without a big lecture or any ranting and raving she simply said, "Do you know how worried and upset I have been waiting for you? I have spent the past two hours wondering if you were dead or alive, and if you *were* alive, how I'd like to kill you! One thin dime (am I dating myself or what?!) and thirty seconds is all it would have taken to check in and out with me about coming home later. I hope you think about that next time."

As usual she was right. The message is as clear and vital today for us as listeners as it was for me thirty years ago.

Make the effort to *Check Things Out*.

*****

I am a mature man reaching 45.

I am a little boy going on 5.

I am independent.

I am so in need of others.

I am hopeful.

I see no answers.

I am competent and resourceful.

I don't think I can do anything.

I have a deep faith.

I can't feel God's presence.

I am fearless.

I am scared.

I am okay.

I am not okay.

And so the list goes on. We are wonderfully complex human beings...multifaceted with sides that we have yet to or may never realize...one day up, another day down...one day this, another day that...one minute experiencing this feeling, another minute experiencing that one.

How great it is to know that there are people in our lives who will listen to and accept these many sides of us.

*****

Thank you is referred to as the magic words and just may be the two most important words in a good listener's vocabulary. When others open up to you they may feel uncomfortable having shared more deeply than they had planned or fearful they took too much of your time. They may be frightened that they entrusted so much to you or be overwhelmed by what they may have seen in themselves.

Expressing our gratitude to the one who confided in us will help to allay some of these fears and plant the seeds for greater sharing, honesty, trust, and intimacy.

Let the speaker know you were touched by her openness,

126

appreciated the trust they placed in you, and that her revelations did not cause you to change your opinion of her (when in fact it has probably been enhanced).

Weren't you taught to say "thank you" when someone gives you a word of praise? What greater compliment than for a person to share herself—the essence of who she is—with you?

*****

Jim was a good friend and a fellow neophyte counseling student. He had a strong desire to become a competent counselor and took quite seriously the admonitions by our teachers to practice this listening stuff throughout our daily routine. There is no one more dangerous than a first-year counseling student!

One evening Jim walked into his apartment to find his wife obviously disturbed from a difficult day at work. It didn't take a Ph.D. to figure this out since she was loudly banging dishes and cabinet doors while preparing dinner in the kitchen!

Having faithfully learned many of the stock responses for such a situation, Jim came out with, "It looks like you've had a frustrating day, honey."

Boom!

"Don't you do that counseling #!*#!* on me!" she exploded.

It might have been a good response for the right person in the right situation, but, uh, not here.

Jim had learned the form and the correct lines but had forgotten rule number one: empathy and understanding is only genuine when it can be demonstrated in action to the person who is hurting. In other words:

Empathy is not empathy unless it hits the mark.

Jim could sense that his wife was struggling. Where it broke down was his inability to genuinely relate this to her. Perhaps a hug would have been a good beginning.

*****

This thing called listening is an art that must be cultivated and practiced continually in order to be done effectively. It may seem phony and uncomfortable for a time. After all, it has been a bit foreign to our natures for much of our life.

Communicating empathy and understanding to others and having it hit home takes some skill and creativity in knowing when and how to do it for each individual speaker. What may be an empathic statement for one may be totally off the mark for another. Although it may be quite genuine, your sincerity might not always be discernible. It takes time.

*****

Increasing our listening skills is exactly like becoming a better singer, mechanic, artist, baseball player, or cook. Without practice and an earnest desire to want to improve, no measurable gains will take place.

At the beginning of each baseball season I remember how foolish I would feel when taking my first swings in the batting cage. They looked like the proverbial rusty-hinged gate and had the punch of hitting with a toothpick rather than a thirty-three-ounce piece of lumber. It was predictable, considering the fact that I had not swung a bat in eight months. My timing eventually returned, but I wonder how much better I would have been if I had worked out with some regularity during the entire year.

And so it is with listening. While taking the summers off, not necessarily by not working but by *choosing* to listen less to people, I found when September came and the students returned to campus and dropped in to talk, my listening abilities were horrendous. I had not practiced these skills for a few months and it was obvious. The duration of my attentiveness had diminished, the amount of advice giving increased, and the capacity to accurately hear and respond to their feelings was often less than effective.

I'm sorry but reading this book is not nearly enough.

You must go and do it...*frequently*!

*****

128

Listeners beware!
You will be labeled.
You will make more friends.
You will be in demand.

*****

Never say, "I'm a lousy listener. I never could listen and I probably never will. It's just not me."

Since listening can indeed be cultivated, what a convenient way of absolving ourselves of any responsibility for wanting to or being capable of hearing another's heart. We rob ourselves of one of the greatest investments we can make in a person's life.

To say, "All I could do was *just* listen to them," does a great injustice to this superb art. By saying "*just*" we relegate the power of the listening ear to such routine tasks as "I'll be right back, I *just* have to go to the store," or "All I had for dinner was *just* a sandwich."

Please do not diminish this beautiful gift to such a level of mediocrity. Let us elevate it to the rightful place of importance it deserves next to such noble concepts as loving, caring, friendship, brotherhood, sisterhood, trust, and respect. It is as precious a commodity as a rare gemstone or priceless antique!

*****

When it is all said and done, they can take away your books, your clothes, your house, your money, and all things material, but they can not take away your ability to listen. Once you sense this vital and dynamic force, you increase your desire to want to do it well and witness first hand its life-enhancing richness. It becomes a part of your being and what makes you you.

Matters of the heart, spirit, and soul are our true life's work and are ours forever. To sense this is the most peaceful of thoughts. Be proud and at home with yourself and this gift you possess. No one can take it away. It is of the eternal.

*****

One of my favorite classes to teach was called "Group Dynamics." This subject was best learned by doing and not through a bunch of stuffy lectures. About twelve students and I met for two hours each week and discussed matters of importance to us—personal, social, academic—you name it.

I was privileged to have an older, more mature student named Betty in one of my groups, who for all practical purposes served as a kind of co-facilitator with me. Each week the students' trust level seemed to grow as Betty asked helpful questions, gave insightful suggestions, and listened with sincere empathy. I ate it up and there were days when I felt like I could actually leave and turn the group over to her.

Then in week eight the proverbial light bulb went on. During each group session many, if not all of the students, expressed at least briefly some of their feelings, thoughts, and concerns. It dawned on me that everyone had shared—except Betty! While she was doing a fantastic job of leading our group, we had yet to hear how and what Betty felt about any subject or issue in relationship to her own life.

At the first opportunity I gently broke in and asked a simple "I'm wondering what you might be thinking and feeling about that, Betty?"

With a look similar to a deer caught in headlights, Betty stammered out, "Ah, oh, um... I don't know. I guess I never really thought much about it."

And so it was. She was at a point in her life where she really didn't think, or feel, or talk about a lot of things close to her.

It's pretty easy to become entangled in the listening trap. The subtle and insidious web we weave by seeking to arrange, sort out, or downright fix the lives of others short circuits our ability to look within. In the long run, it seems much more simple and a lot less painful for me to constantly look outward to your life than inward to mine.

What do you say to working towards *balance*?

130

The Journey

One day you finally knew what you had to do, and
began, though the voices around you kept shouting their
bad advice—

though the whole house began to tremble and you felt the
old tug at your ankles,
Mend my life!" each voice cried.
But you didn't stop. You knew what you had to do,
though the wind pried with its stiff fingers at the very
foundations though their melancholy was terrible.
It was already late enough, and a wild night and the
road full of fallen branches and stones.
But little by little as you left their voices behind, the
stars began to burn through the sheets of clouds and there
was a new voice which you slowly recognized as your
own that kept you company as you strode deeper and
deeper into the world, determined to do the only thing you
could do,
determined to save the only life you could save.

By Mary Oliver

Are you still hiding behind the noble cloak of "I've always been this way and I'm afraid I'll never be able to change."

Then let me share a few lines from an 82-years-young woman who joined me for a workshop on openness, listening, feelings, and relationships:

"Dear Steve,

"The recent seminar at church has made a distinct difference in my life. Change isn't easy to accomplish for someone 82 years old with all those established habits and thought patterns. But, because of this seminar, I have become a more open person. Oh, I'm not running up to strangers and making them bosom companions but I am working on making relationships more open.

"I've extended this effort to my husband and my sister. I intend to reach out to another who attended the seminar for I feel we could be of value to each other..."

Well, good for you! There's no time like the present to consider and commit to becoming more honest, open, and accessible to our thoughts, feelings, and other people. As B. Barton so poignantly said..."*When you're through changing—you're through."*

*****

The river drifts along, oblivious to our life's position or problems. How amazing to think that as we gaze from its banks we will never encounter the same river twice! While flowing along its determined course, the river is ever changing, bringing along a continual fount of new water, never to return again.

If only we could be so in tune with our life's flow—to the natural processes that will take place once we allow ourselves to be open to them. Gifted and compassionate listeners help us to tap into this river and get in sync with its rhythm and its flow.

*****

A woman went to court and told the judge she wanted a divorce.

"Do you have any grounds?" the judge asked.

"Just two acres," she replied.

132

"That's not it, lady. I mean do you have a grudge?"

"No, we park the car in the front of the house."

Frustrated, the judge said, "Does your husband beat you up?"

She replied, "No, I get up before he does."

"Then why do you want a divorce?" the judge asked.

"Because," she confessed...

"We just don't seem able to communicate!"

> * This gem was taken from the Cordele, Georgia Pinecrest Baptist Beacon newsletter.

*****

The Good Book says that

Perfect love casteth out fear.

Fear is probably the most immobilizing force we know. Like a thief, it often robs us of the ability to take risks, make decisions, cultivate true intimacy, and move forward in our lives. *Perfect love* is the only antidote for releasing our fears.

The nearest thing on this earth to *Perfect Love* that I know of? *Listening!*

*****

Your son makes an error and the game is lost.

Your daughter flubs her big line in the class play.

Your spouse messes up the meal for the third day in a row.

Your friend or co-worker makes a mistake that matters little but bothers you.

So, what are you going to do?

How are you going to respond?

With a "You should have...," "You could have...," or "If you only would have..." (the dreaded "Coulda, Woulda, Shoulda" syndrome).

I hope not. If tempted, catch yourself and respond with a simple, "Tough one, eh?," "Sorry...," "It must hurt a little...," or maybe a simple, "Oooops."

Perhaps the best one of all? How about a big hug?

133

*****

If you don't know, don't understand, don't want to misinterpret, and don't want to confuse an issue further, then for gosh sakes, take the brief amount of time and energy needed to CHECK THINGS OUT! It may be the most simple, yet *crucial*, aspect of really tuning into others. Unfortunately we fail to do it with any regularity.

After you finish reading in this book today, your assignment is to take at least <u>three</u> different opportunities to check out something others are expressing or describing to you—no matter how trivial they might seem. There are suggestions of techniques throughout this book on how to best do it. For now, just try it!

*****

One can only wonder how many fewer young people and adults experiencing family, relationship, and personal struggles; school and job dissatisfaction; and feelings of inadequacy there would be...

One can only speculate about how inactive the prisons, jails, and courtrooms would be...

One can only imagine how empty the delinquency centers, detention homes, and principals' offices would be...

One can only guess how much less the pain and how much greater the happiness and fulfillment in our lives would be...

...but for one interested, caring, and committed listener with whom we could have talked while growing up or who we have in our life today.

*****

"If a brother or sister is without clothing and in need of daily food and one of you says to them, 'Go in peace, be warmed and be filled,' and yet you do not give them what is necessary for their body, what use is that?" (James 2:15,16)

If a brother or sister is without an answer or hope for their hurt and in need of a caring listener and one of you says to them, "Go in peace, open up and be listened to," and yet you do not give them what is necessary for their heart and soul, what use is that?

134

Even When It Doesn't Make Sense

Someone pointed out that, logically speaking, if a person is standing with one foot in a tub full of crushed ice and the other foot in a pail of scalding water, "on average" he ought to be comfortable.

Also there was a story of a man who fell into deep water and began thrashing around screaming, "Help me! I can't swim! Save me! I don't know how to swim!" Whereupon a man walking along the edge yelled back in an irritated voice, "Well I can't swim either but you don't hear me carrying on about it, do you?" What is left out of this equation is, of course, the flesh-and-blood experience of the person to whom it is happening.

There is a lot of that to be easily seen in most of the indignant comments and pontifications one hears about the troubles, sufferings, neuroses, and shortcomings of other people: "Wouldn't you think that after all of this time she'd...," "Were I in his situation, you wouldn't find me doing...," "If others can make it there can be no excuse for them not to," etc., etc., etc.

Such appraisals make sense in a way, but much the same kind of sense that it makes to think it okay to average the suffering entailed in having one foot in ice and the other in the boiling water. It is not a failure in logic. (Most of us do very well with logic!)

It is a failure of *empathy*.

*This was taken from the First Congregational "Spire" of Mansfield, Ohio and written by Rev. Cliff Schutjer—a most genuine and fun fellow whose ability to craft a sentence both amazes and inspires me.

Being mentioned in the same breath with him as a wordsmith would be one life's highest compliments!

*****

"But when the Son of Man comes in His glory, and all the angels with Him, then He will sit on His glorious throne.

"Then the King will say to those on His right, 'come, you who are blessed of My Father, inherit the kingdom prepared for you from the foundation of the world.

"For I was hungry, and you gave Me something to eat; I was thirsty, and you gave Me drink; I was a stranger, and you invited Me in; naked, and you clothed Me; I was sick, and you visited Me; I was in prison, and you came to Me.'

"Then the righteous will answer Him, saying, 'Lord, when did we see You hungry, and feed You, or thirsty, and give You drink?

"And when did we see You a stranger, and invite You in, or naked, and clothe You?

"And when did we see You sick, or in prison, and come to You?

"And the King will answer and say to them, 'Truly I say to you, to the extent that you did it to one of these brothers of Mine, even the least of them, you did it to Me.'" (Matthew 25:31, 34-40)

For I was in need of someone to talk to, and you listened to me.

*****

Listening is not merely a set of skills...

...it is a *Continual State of Mind.*

It is a *Lifestyle.*

*****

We look far too much at life in terms of black and white. We leave no room for any of the gray areas.

We tend to generalize our experiences and often take one isolated encounter and in turn apply it to all present and future ones. For example, if my dad always bought Chevrolets or my own experience with a Chevy I purchased was positive, then all Chevrolets will be deemed great and the other auto manufacturers will be judged to be inferior.

If I had a negative interaction with someone from a particular race or religious affiliation, I may then pronounce *all* people from

136

these groups as difficult to deal with or not worthy of my time.

Unfortunately, *one* now becomes *all*. And the sad part is that we miss a real opportunity to enjoy the diversity and richness of life because we categorically dismiss everyone and everything that even remotely relates to what we formerly perceived as a bad experience.

Dare to go beyond these attitudes, pierce the darkness of your biases, and listen with an open and receptive heart.

*****

Consider these terrific words of the great Alfred Adler:

"We can understand and accept ourselves realistically only when someone outside of ourselves first understands and accepts us."

That takes a good listener, my friend.

*****

It is said that a fish spends so much time in water that he does not even know he's in it. What a perfect analogy for the human condition when it comes to pain, problems, and unhealthy situations.

A good listener can help us to feel the sensation of being wet, recognize we're in the water, and possibly keep us from drowning in it.

*****

A favorite Family Circus cartoon shows Jeffy admonishing his scowling little brother and sister: "Grandma says of all the things you wear, your expression is the most important."

And so it is when listening.

*****

When asked if there was anything worse than being blind, the marvelous Helen Keller answered, "Yes! Being able to see and having no vision." May I be so presumptuous as to assume her answer to the following question?

"Ms. Keller, could there be anything worse than being deaf"?

"Yes there is," she might respond. *"Being able to hear but unable to truly LISTEN!"*

137

*****

An old English proverb...
"The best mirror is an old friend"
*****

A good friend (and good listener) is someone with whom
you don't have to worry about making sense all of the time.
Friends are people who like you even after they get to know you!
What a relief to have people with whom you can just be yourself.
*****

Passed on to me were the following words:
*"Let me not dilute the effectiveness of the help
I can give by letting it take the form of giving advice."*
*****

Telling a poor listener or one who is detached and distracted to
"please hear me"
can be a lot like chastising a short person to just get taller!
*****

The *greatest legacy* we can leave our children and loved ones
are memories. And aren't some of life's most vivid, warm, and
lasting remembrances those which involve a time of listening and
connecting?

*****

When we expend so much time and effort keeping in and
holding on to our anger, *we lower the voltage of our entire life.*

We can only access a portion of our energy because most of it
is being utilized just to manage and keep a lid on the anger.

*****

I was attending a meeting with one of my favorite
supervisors—a man who was a *great* listener. Actually, in
retrospect, all of my favorite supervisors and bosses were excellent
listeners. They made an earnest attempt to hear and acknowledge
me. I guess that's what made them my favorites.

The meeting was with a rather verbose and often aloof fellow
who unfortunately represented a major funding source for our

138

agency. After being machine gunned by his rapid-fire, non-stop verbiage for sixty minutes, the meeting concluded. As we were heading back to our offices, Dave turned to me and said, "Steve, do you know what that man's problem is?"

Having a few hunches of my own, I was most interested to hear Dave's.

"He listens with his mouth!"

*****

When I speak on the topic of listening, I am invariably stopped by someone at a break, during lunch time, or after the conclusion of a workshop. On more than one occasion, it has been a man or woman lamenting the fact that their spouse or a significant other was not attending the workshop. After all, "he's the one who could *really* use it! I'm a pretty good listener myself," the person proclaims.

After hearing them recite a relentless litany of wishes for their partner to change, open up more, talk, feel, and do who knows what else, I sometimes began to feel emotionally and physically drained. I could not help but wonder how overwhelmed these people must feel when confronted daily by these "good listeners."

Quite honestly, there have been times when it was all I could do to keep from saying to them, "Have you ever kept quiet (or shut up) long enough to hear what they might be trying to say?!?"

*****

An inordinate amount of time and energy is often spent nurturing our material possessions. We do not think twice about the hours spent taking care of the car, fixing up our house, accumulating a wardrobe, perfecting favorite hobbies, or doing something just right.

Sadly it often pales in comparison with the disproportionately feeble quantity of time and energy we allocate for the care of our body, soul, spirit, and relationships. Just think what kind of shape they would be in if we paid them similar attention and gave them equal importance.

139

The following is excerpted from a wonderful little book entitled *The Tao of Leadership* by John Heider.

KNOWING WHAT IS HAPPENING

When you cannot see what is happening in a group [or the life of another], do not stare harder. Relax and look gently with your inner eye.

When you do not understand what a person is saying, do not grasp for every word. Give up your efforts. Become silent inside and listen with your deepest self.

When you are puzzled by what you see or hear, do not strive to figure things out. Stand back for a moment and become calm.

When a person is calm,

complex events appear simple.

To know what is happening, push less, open out and be aware. See without staring. Listen quietly rather than listening hard. Use intuition and reflection rather than trying to figure things out.

The more you can let go of trying, and the more open and receptive you become, the more easily you will know what is happening.

Also, stay in the present. The present is more available than either memories of the past or fantasies of the future.

So attend to what is happening now.

(*Italics* mine)

*****

Left unattended or unresolved, our feelings strike a dissonant chord that rings throughout our words and behavior.

Being open to the natural stages or progression of their expression allows us to heal them more quickly and fully. Coming to terms with the feelings we continue to accumulate and harbor increases the amount of quality time we can spend in the here and now. After all, the only thing we truly have is the present.

Relinquishing the negative power we often give to our feelings and listening to their message and meaning, they now enlighten and accompany us on our journey as a *friend* and *companion*.

*****

Feelings are the primary way we relate to ourselves.
And if we do not learn to be more open and receptive to them,
how can we truly connect with and relate to another?

*****

Many of the addictions, diseases, physical ills, and times of loneliness and discontent have their roots in the inability to get close to and be at home with ourselves. We become separated from and often medicate our feelings.

Families pay a steep price when the emotional climate is established that "we do not *talk feelings* in this house." Or, it could be that "only *certain feelings are okay* to discuss." There may even be two or more sets of "feelings rules" for different family members. For instance, feelings that are okay for father or son to express are not acceptable for mother or daughter to discuss.

Sharing feelings develops a sense of connection. The seeds this sows for our children's future relationships are potent.

*****

Accessing and staying current with our feelings heightens communication and intimacy with God and others, as well as with ourselves. They affirm our humanity and are the glue that bonds all relationships, making us kindred spirits.

*****

141

GOD, WHEN I

Look

Help Me To Truly See

When I Question

Help Me To Actually Discover

When I Hope

Help Me To Genuinely Believe

When I Feel

Help Me To Fully Experience

When I Speak

Help Me To Honestly Express Myself

When I Reach Out

Help Me To Gently Touch

When I Turn Things Over

Help Me To Really "Let Go"

When I Hear

Help Me To Sincerely LISTEN

Steve Powers, 1990

*****

We discover ourselves when we listen to our inner voice.

*****

Acknowledging, listening to, and flowing with our feelings
will free up our life's energy and move us towards
greater clarity, direction, and peace.

*****

Instead of spending needless time attempting
to avoid, minimize, or running from our feelings,
why not consider *running to* a listening ear?

*****

Our four-year-old daughter, Elizabeth, has little trepidation
when entering the world of feelings or asking the tough questions.
One evening she and my wife, Sue, were chatting about "Dot Dot,"
a dear and long-time friend who was to babysit her the next day.
During the course of the discussion, Elizabeth asked about Dot's
husband and discovered that he had died many years ago.

Upon Dot's arrival, Elizabeth began playing with her and
before long began to talk about what she had learned the previous
evening. With her most sincere look and expression of concern
she told Dot that she was very sorry to hear about her husband.
Her next few words brought tears to all of our eyes when she said,
"Who cried with you, Dot Dot?"

*****

I was busy in the office one morning, more than likely just re-
stacking the many piles I create, when my then four year-old-son
Jeremy came barreling into the room, looked me straight in the
eye, and asked, "Are you happy, Dad?"

The question stopped me dead in my tracks. Now does he
mean "happy" happy as in happy all the time? In general, overall,
most of the time happy? Or, just happy right now?

Well, if you know anything about kids his age he meant happy
right now.

Not wanting to make a major commitment as to how I was

143

feeling (after all, it was still early morning and the day was young) I responded with a rather weak, "Ah, yeah, Jeremy. I guess I am kinda happy."

His response?

"Then why don't you tell your face, Dad?!!"

That sure got my attention—as if to say "You could have fooled me by what you were expressing on your face and body." The same holds so very true for genuine listening.

*****

"Are you *really listening* to me?"

"Ah, yeah, sure I am."

"Then why don't you tell your face?!?"

*****

Interesting research about personal attraction to other people lends much credence to the power of a listener's non-verbal cues.

7% of our attraction is based on liking *what* one says.

38% is connected to *how* it is said, and

55% is related directly to *facial* and *non-verbal expressions*.

What our body communicates for good or ill is often the most potent stimulus and punctuation to the words we say and the message we send. Simply stated, it lets the speaker know whether you are interested or not. It either encourages him to *keep going* or abruptly tells him "conversation over."

*****

While growing up one of my favorite game shows was "It's Not What You Say, It's What You Don't Say." Never were truer words spoken about the listening process.

It's often what a person does *not* say, can only *hint* at, or *leaves out completely* that speaks volumes.

Take for example the child who describes her mom for an hour and never mentions her dad; the husband who talks admiringly about his family but fails to mention his wife; the teacher who discusses her classroom and each child and forgets about little Sarah; and the person who details the feelings and

144

experiences of others but says very little about his own.

Despite the clear absence of a certain person or a gap in one's story, it may not be so obvious to the speaker. The missing piece might be a topic too painful to bring up or one that is unwittingly buried in a safe compartment.

A good listener is willing to
gently inquire about the unspoken.

*****

I get a tad defensive when someone accuses counselors and helping professionals of having a soft, easy job. I've heard "and you get paid for doing that?!?" too many times.

Usually it is said by a person who has a physical type of job. I sometimes respond with, "Oh, yeah. I sure do. Why don't you go home tonight and listen to your spouse intently and without interruption for at least fifteen minutes? Or try being interested and involved without saying much for about 5-10 minutes with three different co-workers today! Oh, and try doing both of those things for *an entire day* while mixing in the preoccupying thoughts and pain of your own problems as well as theirs while you're at it. Now tell me how easy it is, okay?"

Shuts 'em right up!!

*****

If I were to tell each one of you reading this book that you possessed something which gives you the ability to connect with others; to build trust in relationships; to sort out a little of this often complicated thing called life; to gain respect and mutual support among your colleagues, co-workers, or employees; to empower others; to work out problems; to feel happier, more hopeful, less stressed, and more in tune with yourself; and to have more energy—you might ask me, "Does it come in a liquid, powder, capsule, pill, or needle?!"

No, my friend.

It takes form in the shape of your ears, eyes, and heart.

*****

Please, Do Not Attempt This At Home!

WARNING: Do not try the following experiment at home! And don't even think about doing it with me, okay?

It seems that a senior psychology college class had the brilliant idea of how to dramatically portray the power of non-verbal communication. They called together a group of young students who were taking the rather boring, but required, Psychology 101. Professor Smith had been teaching the *same course* for twenty-eight years! His notes, which were originally penned on white paper, had now yellowed with age. He stood behind a lectern and in full monotone, read to his very uninspired audience.

Barely looking up, except to check the time or take a short respite, he plodded through the lectures. Day after day he droned on, without expression or emotion. The students had no choice but to show up since their grades were largely determined by attendance and the tests were filled with exacting details from his lectures. On to the "experiment."

Professor Smith's students were asked by the advanced class for one week to utilize every listening and attending skill they knew during his lectures. If he even hinted at something funny, they were to smile or laugh. They were instructed to ask questions and make comments, to nod their heads, throw in a few "mmm's" and "uh huhs," and to always practice the "SOLER SYSTEM":

S = *Squarely face* the speaker

O = Keep an *Open posture*

L = Slightly *Lean forward* towards the speaker

E = Maintain good *Eye contact*, and

146

R = Be as *Relaxed* as possible. *Remember:* Your comfort level is in direct proportion and linked to the content of what the speaker is telling you.

(In case you are wondering, yes, we covered another version of the SOLER system in a different part of this book. And, no, I am not putting it in twice because I need to fill a certain amount of pages: it's just that I hope you will sense how very important I think this is to the art of listening. Hey, you may even find it a third time too!

By the second and third day of this experiment, Professor Smith was literally changing before their very eyes—a complete metamorphosis. He actually greeted students as they entered the classroom. No longer content to lecture behind a podium, he now began moving freely about from one side to the other. Animated, using voice inflections, sharing stories left untold for years, a sparkle now replaced the glaze in his eyes.

He began to feel things inside he had not experienced since his early years of teaching. He felt alive, with a renewed sense of purpose. Teaching was becoming fun and fulfilling again, all because there were students who seemed interested in and found important what he had to say.

Sadly, a few weeks later, the students were asked to complete the experiment and return to their former mode of interaction. With their frequent stares out of windows, little meaningful contact, heads bowed, and yawns intermixed, Professor Smith once again moved back behind the podium to feebly read his notes. A rather sad tale indeed but...

Such awesome power, this listening ear!

*****

Listening not only has the ability to inform...

...but also to transform an attitude, perception, and one's reality.

*****

Sales people, marketing personnel, and consultants would be wise to *overdevelop* one skill—*Listening.*

By demonstrating a sincere interest in their client—truly hearing the concerns, deciphering their needs, and relating person to person—everyone would benefit. There would be a greater likelihood of satisfaction for all involved. Come to think of it, the same would hold true for just about everyone—supervisors, administrators, bosses, teachers, co-workers, and loved ones!

*****

A film critic began his radio report with the following sound bytes from four folks who had just attended a popular new movie:

"It was the best movie I have ever seen!"

"It was the worst movie I ever saw!"

"It was okay but seemed to drag a lot. Pretty slow moving."

"It was great! End to end action throughout."

No wonder it's so tough getting on the same page with others!

*****

As the French philosopher Voltaire said so beautifully:

"The road to the heart is through the ear."

*****

The German Theologian Paul Tillich reminds us that:

"The first duty of love is to listen."

*****

I once had the opportunity and privilege to make regular presentations to the men at the Ohio State Reformatory. They were in the pre-release program and many would be leaving prison within days or weeks.

My walk up the sidewalk was always an inexorably long one, filled with anxiety and doubt. I was not afraid of the setting or the men but wondered whether I had anything meaningful to say during my two-hour presentation. After all, what could I possibly relate to these men that they did not already know. Furthermore, who was I to think that they would even take seriously my thoughts and ideas—a complete stranger from the "outside."

Each visit I entered with these feelings. Every time I left, I came out with renewed hope, a connection with these men, and new light within myself. As I began to open up with them, they in turn did with me. The more we talked, the more we found we had in common.

During one particularly poignant moment, I looked out at this group of very accepting individuals and these words just popped out of my mouth. "You know, guys, it has suddenly dawned on me that there is little difference between me and you when it comes to our emotional and spiritual lives. I have come to realize that in many areas of my life I have put up steel and walls too.

"This prison has nothing to do with a physical cell block made from concrete. It has to do with closing down my feelings, losing touch with my spiritual self, and my unwillingness to do what I need to do to grow."

At that point I saw some heads nod, smiles appear, and even heard an "amen" or two. One of the men gave a wink and said, "You know, Steve, for the last couple of years in here I have never felt and been more free. I have come to understand that once I got past the bars and walls, I had to deal with the ones in my own heart and soul. Yeah, I'm a little scared about getting out, but for the first time I have hope. I am so thankful for the people who have taken the time to *listen* and help me do some renovation work on the inside."

*****

Is there anything more horrendous than a debilitating toothache, headache, backache, earache, or chronic condition that causes pain to dominate your life? As this pain continues or intensifies, how sensitive are you to another's feelings or concerns? Not too, I'm sure.

In general we become preoccupied with one thing—lessening or getting rid of the pain we are experiencing. We're thinking of a doctor, treatment, or remedy. "Just get me out of this pain" is often our predominant thought and plea.

It's tough to be concerned about another's dilemma when our own is *screaming* so loudly to us—seemingly shouting our name.

As we discover ways to appropriately and healthfully manage, heal or live with our inner pain, we are much better able to let another person's in. Only then can we really hear what they are trying to tell us.

*****

Frequent flyers have the bad habit of tuning out the flight attendant as she dutifully recites the safety procedures. I am guilty as charged.

On one particular flight, however, an attendant's manner of speaking really captured my attention. She was just finishing the part about the seat cushions transforming themselves into flotation devices in the unlikely event of a water landing. (Very reassuring words when flying from Cleveland to Philadelphia because the only water you spot is in a backyard pool in Pittsburgh. You suddenly see yourself in a made-for-TV movie rescuing fellow passengers from the deep end!)

Now came the final directive. This one had to do with these magical masks that would drop from the compartment above if our airplane cabin lost oxygen. Her closing sentence was a gem and hit at the heart of the issue of becoming a good listener.

"Ladies and gentlemen. If you are accompanying a child *or* someone in need of your help and assistance, *in order that you may better be able to take care of that person, please take care of yourself first.*"

Whoa! Is that deep or what? Especially for only a flight from Cleveland to Philly! We listen best and more completely to others when we seek to earnestly listen to and take proper care of ourselves. *Our positive feelings can't help but flow out to others.*

150

Healthy and whole people do genuinely caring
and healthy things for others! It just seems to come naturally.
*****

If you have ever been a commuter, you certainly will relate to the times when you were not sure how you got to work, the commuter blackouts you experienced, and any number of bizarre incidents you witnessed or, in which you were in fact involved.

I proudly bought a shiny older gray and black sedan that had certainly once had its day. Unfortunately, none of those days were when I owned it! The car spent about the same amount of time on the road as it did in the shop. The latest ailment to befall it was a broken speedometer. When I heard the repair estimate, I figured, "Hey, who needs a speedometer?"

For the next several months I made the hour-long drive with no problems. The speed and trip just felt right. I had gotten to know the car pretty well and it was as if I could measure the correct speed by certain engine sounds, wind noise, and a feeling in my gut.

The day came when I had saved enough to purchase a more reliable vehicle and sell the sedan. I had a friend follow me the fifty miles to the car dealership. When we got there I asked her, "So, how fast were we going?"

"55 mph on the highway and 25-35 mph through the little towns," she said.

"Right on the mark," I thought to myself.

Now if only I could do that same kind of listening with the more important areas of my life—in my heart and soul.
*****

As I opened the door for my mom to exit the mall (just as she had always taught me to do), she paused for a second, looked me in the eye, and asked, "Hey, Steve, before we leave for the other mall, do you have to go to the bathroom?"

After picking up the bottom half of my mouth, furrowing my brow and pondering for a moment, I let out a barely audible "Uh,"

151

"Hmm" and responded with an, "Ah, no Mom. I think I'm okay."
Neither of us even batted an eyebrow!

Not an unusual exchange between a mom and her four-year-old son. The only problem? I was 35, and she was 63! Knowing we could easily digress here to the subject of "moms will always be moms" and "kids will always be kids," let me just make the following point.

I, like you, have become fairly adept at listening to certain parts of my life. I have developed the art of knowing when I need to use a bathroom. Normal eaters (yes, there are some out there!) know when they are hungry or when they are full. Conditioned and responsive athletes know what to do and when to do it. Good parents know when to push their kids or when to best let go. You've got the idea...

What I am suggesting is that we take more time to consider how we might discover and develop ways to not only listen better to others, but just as important, to hear what our own feelings and spirit are wanting to say to us.

*****

It is fascinating to read the research on communication styles—particularly about men and women. Enough data exists to support the notion of differences in brain physiology and processing of feelings. There is "left brain" vs. "right brain" and, as I have observed in human behavior, "half brain," "no brain," "numb brain," and "do you have any brains at all brain?"

Whatever the case, be it nature and/or nurture, men and women do seem to have a different take on feelings, relationships, and communication. In general, women are viewed to be more open and comfortable with feelings and matters of the heart than we men. In fact, if given the choice, some men would probably choose a root canal without pain killers over talking about feelings! We're getting a little better but we still have a way to go.

Ladies, may I pick on you a bit now? Do not fool yourselves into thinking that because you are good at describing feelings

152

from a present or previous experience that you are necessarily in touch with, working out, or healing those particular feelings.

There is a big difference in talking <u>about</u> one's emotions and talking <u>in</u> them. In spending most of our time talking *about* feelings we tend to detach from or intellectualize them. While talking *in* our feelings, we move towards increased identification, ownership, and healing.

We obviously cannot talk in our feelings all the time or chaos would probably reign. But we need to challenge ourselves to be aware of the differences between talking *about* and *in* the emotions and how we can more appropriately begin to deal with them.

*****

We live much of our lives from the neck up.

Detached and sometimes oblivious to what is going on within, we seem resolved and content to simply go about *doing*. The doing mode is our effort at keeping the status quo and not risking any openness or change.

For those of you who frequent your local churches, take note of the choir. It may sometimes be a clue as to how open and receptive the pastor, church, and congregation are to feelings.

A church where a range of feelings are welcome and expressed often has a choir whose singers move to the beat of the music, sway to the rhythm, and smile broadly when singing songs of hope and gratitude.

I have been in churches where only certain emotions are okay, openness is a struggle or not encouraged, and feelings always take a back seat to faith. Many in the choir often sing with restraint— even songs which proclaim peace and great things for the future. Beneath their flowing robes, very little moves.

Just like pain and joy, faith and feelings can and do co-exist. They are very much two sides of the same coin. Good listeners help us to see and have the freedom to live in both.

*****

153

"Did You Even Get A Hold Of George?"

I was particularly proud of how hard I had worked to help my friend. Her plate was overflowing with a week of term papers and final exams. Although busy myself, I decided that my situation was a bit more manageable and less stressful than hers. So, on my lunch breaks and squeezed between appointments, I was able to take care of the many tasks that she was unable to complete.

At the end of the week I received a little note from her. Expecting to read a few words of thanks, shock and anger would best describe my feelings at what she wrote. It simply said, "Steve, did you even get a hold of George this week?" Among the many items on her "to do" list was to contact her friend George.

"Did I even get a hold of George? How dare you ask that! I took care of every item on the list, and then some. And you have the nerve to ask me, did I even get a hold of George? Some gratitude."

I sat on these feelings for several days. I still couldn't believe she would say that. Finally, the time seemed right and I broached the topic. "Hey, you know that note you left me last week about calling George? I really can't believe you asked, 'Did I even get a hold of George?'—especially after all I did to help you out. That really hurt my feelings."

"What are you talking about? I didn't write 'Did you even get a hold of George?' I wrote 'Did you <u>ever</u> get a hold of George?' It was just intended as a reminder to call him, or if you did, to let me know what you found out. I really appreciated all you did for me!"

Funny thing. Her "r"s and "n"s look suspiciously similar—especially when she was writing in a hurry. Do you realize how much grief and turmoil I would have been spared if I had had the courage to simply *clarify* what I thought was in her note. The days after reading it probably took two months off my life because of all the feelings I was stuffing and allowing to eat away at me.

Good listeners have the gumption and chutzpah to *check things out!* It's a must...

*****

Have you ever poured out your heart to someone, wanting and asking *only* to be listened to, and found yourself bombarded with a variation of any of the following?

> •*"Cheer up! It'll get better in time."*
> •*"I know (or understand) just how you feel!"*
> •*"You shouldn't feel that way!"*

When I am met with any of these responses, I usually either say "thanks, I'll see you later" or just quietly walk away. It feels like a punch in the stomach, as if the proverbial wind has been taken out of your sails. You muster up the gumption to express a feeling, fear, or painful event and get something which is worse than nothing—another's judgment, misplaced empathy, or empty encouragement.

Sure, maybe, hopefully it will *get better in time.*

But I cannot see that at this moment.

Right now I need to feel, to grieve, to hurt—*to just be.*

Do you really know and understand *"just how I feel?"*

You mean the anger and issues you had in your broken relationship were exactly like mine? The feelings and dynamics related to your job loss or the death of your mother were just like mine? And the fears and concerns you have about your troubled teenager are no different than those that I have? I don't think so. Similar. Perhaps very similar. But please try not to assume "just how I feel."

Oh, and so I *"shouldn't feel this way,"* huh?

How should I feel? Like you think you would or I should?

Right now I just need to feel. There will be plenty of time to sort out how rational or appropriate my feelings are. If I can't tell you any of my feelings—warts, silly notions, and all— then I can't release the sting in my secrets, and the power they hold over me. Just hang in there with me and perhaps you can help me with the excavation and the challenging work of understanding—*later.*

*****

I wish that grieving and forgiving were only one-time or short-term events. They are, however, most often a life-long process. Our grief over a significant loss is generally ongoing, and our forgiving of another is usually best described as "forgive and forgive" and not "forgive and forget."

Each time we feel a twinge of the hurt or a twinge of the pain is still another invitation for us to do some more healing. Humanly speaking, no loss can ever be fully replaced or resolved nor every wrong completely righted. But through the compassion of God, the ears of another, and the courage we can summon from within, the process comes closer to completion and closure.

*****

Simply being with someone during emotionally overpowering times is often the greatest way we can be of help to them. Consider providing arms of comfort, ears of support, and tears of shared pain.

*****

One of the greatest skills we can develop as a friend, parent, loved one, worker, salesperson, boss, or helping professional is that of being a good listener. One of the greatest attributes we may bring to any relationship is that of being *genuine* with all that it implies—sincerity, honesty, openness to feelings, caring, being "real," balanced...

It's about maintaining a certain measure of vulnerability while developing a healthy portion of inner strength. My good friend Susan once coined a word for genuine people. They have a sense of "spontanuity" in their lives—a combination of *continuity* and consistency mixed with a liberal dose of *spontaneity* and openness to life's richness.

In short, a genuine person works at knowing and being comfortable with himself—warts and all! And in turn, he has no problem being congruent and expressing on the *outside* what is taking place on the *inside*.

156

*****

Gerard Egan in his superb book *The Skilled Helper* states that genuineness in one's relationships is another way of showing a person respect. He gives a great list of characteristics for helping professionals which, when slightly adapted, is pertinent for *all* listeners:

• Not changing who you are when interacting with different people

• Not constantly adopting new roles and ways of interacting in order to be acceptable to others

• Relating deeply to others as a part of our lifestyle and not just hats we put on or take off at will

• Developing the ability to express directly to another whatever we are presently experiencing (this is being congruent)

• Communicating without distorting messages (being concrete)

• Listening to others without distorting their messages (the crux of this book in a nutshell!)

• Revealing our true motivations as we communicate our message

• Being spontaneous and free in our communications with others rather than using habitual or planned strategies and methods

• Responding more immediately to another's feelings and current state rather than waiting for or worrying about the right time or coming up with the right answer

• Living and communicating in the here and now

• Learning how to enjoy emotional/psychological closeness

• Striving for interdependence rather than dependence or counter dependence in our relationships

Be mindful that the above traits should always be cloaked in the garb of compassion, tact, balance, and whatever is most helpful and appropriate for the speaker.

*****

157

Father John Powell has been like a mentor to me through his wonderful books and videos. His classic book *Why Am I Afraid to Tell You Who I Am* lends insight into the arena of openness and feelings. In one sentence, a young man so beautifully answers the question Father Powell's book title asks of all of us:

"Because if I tell you who I am, you might not like who I am, and that's all that I have."

Wow! Our feelings indeed make up *who* we are.

In essence, *we are our feelings.*

Not to be aware of, listen to, understand, express, and heal our feelings is to only be partially alive. They are the primary way we relate to ourselves and if we cannot access what is within, how can we connect on a deep or meaningful level with another?

*****

I have alluded to the importance of healthy listeners taking better care of themselves—especially in the areas of proper nutrition, rest, and fitness. Why not try combining two great needs towards improved physical and emotional health? Walk and talk with a buddy. Make and share healthful meals and conversation with one another. Join the "Y" or a fitness center and work out your bodies, emotions, and souls at the same time!

*****

Good friends and good listeners are those who provide both support and reality checks. "Reality checks" are the result of having someone a bit more objective than yourself to either confirm or present a different perspective about your feelings or your experiences.

For example, you have really hopped on the treadmill of life and can't seem to get off. Many of your actions have straddled the line of being irrational. You say to your friend, "I think I'm going crazy." He provides a reality check and says, "Yup. I think you are too!" Whoops!!

On another occasion you may have a job, home, or relationship where there is a person with a significant problem (chemical dependency, eating disorder, abuse, temper, emotionally distant, etc.). She accuses you of certain things, often blaming you for her behavior, and you begin to buy into some of it.

After discussing some of these feelings and issues with a good friend, you still wonder "is it all me?" In providing a reality check, the listener begins to take your conversation apart and show you what are genuinely your problems and what are the problems of the other person.

Relieved, you may finally come to realize: "This is really her problem, not mine. I need to stop taking all of it on!"

Good friends and listeners are ones who are willing to lend us an ear or give us a kick. They see things we can't or won't see and know how to kindly tell us about them.

*****

Could it be that the struggle in expressing our feelings is rooted in the fact that many times we do not even *know what* we are feeling?

We have become so adept over the years in separating ourselves from our feelings that being asked to verbalize them may be akin to asking a person to fly. Impossible! A listening ear or two may begin to move a person closer to his feelings.

*****

Denial is often the most automatic, subtle, and pervasive of all defenses. Simply stated, denial, like all of the defenses we employ, serves to separate us from our hurt and feelings in order to protect us from the pain.

Denial, however, is not necessarily a negative thing. It gives us some insulation and protection from potentially debilitating or immobilizing feelings and experiences.

I am writing these words after having just spent the past week along with the rest of America watching in horror, shock, anger, and great sadness as the victims of the Oklahoma City bombing tragedy attempt to pick up the pieces of their shattered lives.

We have repeatedly heard the words emanating from their

hearts: "I still can't believe this has happened" or "This hasn't really hit me yet."

Thank God for denial and the ability to get some distance from this excruciating pain. In time, often with help and love, the denial will fade and true healing may begin.

Denial is a concern when we become entrenched in it, and it accompanys us like a faithful partner. It is the single greatest force which keeps us from seeing the problems and pain of another, our family, and ourselves. Denial helps to keep us functioning and intact. But like many of the "friendships" we develop such as with food, smoking, crazy relationships, drinking, drugging, over working, busyness, etc., it eventually turns against us.

Without the ability to see our lives, feelings, and actions more honestly and accurately, we become victimized and burdened by the entrapped pain and treadmill of denial. Sometimes it is only a crisis, a time of hitting bottom, or the powerful ears of another which can penetrate these defenses.

*****

When my son Jeremy was two-and-a-half-years-old he was tightly fastened in his familiar back seat location as we went tooling down the highway. Mindlessly humming the radio's tunes and thinking my son was babbling at the passing scenery, I paid little attention and drove obliviously on.

After a piercing shout, I peered in the rearview mirror to see his beet red face glaring right at me.

"Talk to me, Dad!" he yelled at me. "Talk to me!!"

Translation...

"Listen to me, Dad! Listen to me!!"

*****

Beginning a sentence with "I think that..." may be a common and convenient way for us to not really own what we are feeling.

Couched in the "I think that..." we talk in enough generalities to avoid experiencing any major rejection.

Communicating on an "I feel" basis says to ourselves and

160

another: "I own and accept responsibility for what I am about to tell you." Small word change. *Big shift!*

*****

Try living by the "84 - 12 - 4 - 2 - 1/2 formula for life."

They did a study on the topic of worry and the things that preoccupy a person's thoughts and time. (By the way, often having heard countless speakers, teachers, and writers refer to "They did a study on..." I finally discovered who "They" were. "They" are two guys in a tiny town and office in Kansas called "They, Inc." That's who "They" is!). It goes like this...

•*84%* of the things we worry about *never happen.*

•*12%* happens but we have *no control* over it.

•We can control or change only *4%* of what we worry about and which actually *happens.*

•The *"2"* in our equation represents the joy and positives in our life which become doubled when shared with another.

•The *"1/2"* is the pain and worry that when listened to gets cut in half. Literally, its potency and ability to dominate our thoughts and lives is diminished and reduced.

*****

Synergy is one of those words (like "affirmation") that says so much to me just by hearing it spoken. The Greek roots and definition of this word denote a sense of new and regenerated energy which develops when two separate entities join forces.

This, my friends, is what true listening is all about: two or more people who connect and give one another a revitalized sense of hope, energy, and new direction. Awesome!

*****

Here is a great description of "blocks" we maintain that keep us from listening. The list is taken from *Messages: The Communication Book.*

Which ones do you recognize yourself doing?

1. Comparing—"I earn more than that"... "My kids are brighter"... "He hasn't had it as tough as I have"...

161

2. Mind reading—"She says she wants to go, but I'll bet she's tired"... "I'll bet he's looking at my lousy skin"...

3. Rehearsing—"I'll say... then he'll say... then I'll say"...

4. Filtering—Only paying attention long enough to see if that person is angry, unhappy, etc., then letting your mind wander.

5. Judging—Prejudging someone as nuts, stupid, or unqualified before hearing what they have to say.

6. Dreaming—Half-listening, flashing off on your own chain of private associations.

7. Identifying—Taking everything someone tells you and referring it back to your own experience.

8. Advising—Problem solving, fixing, or suggesting rather than simply hearing the other person.

9. Sparring—Arguing, debating, putting others down, or discounting.

10. Being right—Going to any length to avoid being wrong, not being able to take suggestions or to be corrected, or to listen to criticism.

11. Derailing—Suddenly changing the subject, joking it off to avoid the conversation.

12. Placating—Agreeing with everything rather than tuning in and really hearing what's being said.

*****

I once worked with a very respected psychologist who had perfected a great skill I called the "smoke the pipe, be quiet, and let 'em hang themselves" technique. You would enter his impeccable office and find an empty desktop, save for a pipe and stand. As the discussion evolved and natural silences occurred, he would puff more and more on his pipe—lit or unlit.

Smart man. Not only was this relaxing, but it also kept him from giving into the temptation to interrupt the thought processes of the one speaking.

I can't tell you how many times a short visit to see him with the intention of discussing a minor item turned into a much deeper conversation. His comfortableness with silence and his ability to be patient were like an unwritten invitation to talk. It was amazing to see what all was inside, waiting to be asked out!

If you want to try this technique, keep a non-toxic, slightly smaller-than-your-mouth object next to you. When you get the urge to break the silence or to give another a piece of outstanding advice, stuff it in your mouth. If that's a bit too vivid, then just touch your hand to your mouth—or even cover it! That will do the trick!!

*****

There are times when people in our life need to be confronted about something. However, there is a much better chance of getting our message through if we lay a groundwork of listening, empathy, and understanding. By being willing to walk in the proverbial moccasins of another, we begin to *earn the right* to challenge him.

Hey, don't tell me what you think is wrong or what I need to do until you have first shown me that you care about me in other ways—namely, with your ears and heart. I then may not only be more open to what you have to say but actually feel more comfortable asking for your feedback when I need it.

*****

A highlight for any teacher, parent, helping professional, fellow worker, or friend is to get a note of thanks or having a person tell you how much you have helped him.

We were finishing up the first day of a two-day workshop with a group of teachers on what else but listening! The homework assignment that evening was to become involved in some talking/listening situations and take note of the amount and type of listening/non listening taking place—especially on the teachers' part!

The next morning we circled up and I asked the question, "So what did you learn about yourself last evening?"

We heard many encouraging and insightful responses from the

163

participants about their listening level and awareness. Then Kathy raised her hand and said, "Right now I'm really tired. But it's a good kind of tired."

She went on to describe how she had stayed up until two a.m. with her 20-year-old daughter. Apparently at about 10 p.m. she had posed the question to her, "So what kind of a listener do you think I am, honey?"

In four hours she had her answer and a whole lot more. Things were talked about that they had both wanted to discuss for years but were unable or too afraid to bring up. They talked, hugged, cried, and even yelled—and then talked some more.

"Mom," she said. "I really feel like you heard me tonight."

Kathy told our class, "I think she's right. We connected like we have never connected before." And it was all because Kathy took the risk to become calm within, to temper the urge to defend herself, and to *listen.*

Are you willing to ask those people close to you in your life, "So what kind of a listener do you think I am?" While it may open a Pandora's box, it might also uncover some buried treasures!

*****

Don't you just love it when people break in at mid-sentence and proceed to finish your thought? It's bad enough when they complete it with some semblance of accuracy, even worse when they miss the mark.

As wise King Solomon says, *"He who gives an answer before he hears, it is folly and shame to him."*

*****

Have you ever gotten into a full blown argument over the toothpaste cap being left off or had a major disagreement about where to eat dinner?

Being angry or obsessed over a situation far out of proportion to its relative importance usually means there is something else going on. The abandoned cap or eating location are not the actual issues. A good listener can help us discover the real story.

164

*****

I needed my birth certificate one day and began to ponder where it might be. Looking for it elicited warm memories of my mom, because my mom had a place for everything and everything was in its place. She was not compulsive about neatness, rather she just took an orderly and common sense approach to life.

"Where would my mom keep a birth certificate?" I asked myself. "Probably in a locked safety deposit box," I thought.

Since I did not have a bank safety deposit box, I headed for the next closest thing—a fireproof security box in the basement.

I turned the key, opened the lid, and there it was laying right on top: a white envelope labeled "Steve's Birth Certificate" written in my mom's beautiful cursive script. The tears began to flow as a flood of pain and memories poured over me. Although we had buried my mother more than two years before, the sadness of her being gone was still very real. Remember, grieving is a process that knows no end.

I'm glad I had some people I could tell this story to and not feel weak, inferior, or ashamed. The legacy of loved ones is kept alive in our heart and soul through memories. We won't incur the risk of blocking out those wonderful memories if we refuse the urge to hold in the pain of our loss.

*****

"Hey Steve, I need to talk with you. Soon!" Teri shouted as she stood about five feet from my face.

"Okay Teri, chill. How about 3:00 today," I replied.

"That would be great," she said.

Teri was a senior social work major I had had in several classes since her freshman year. She could best be described as being sincere, mature, outgoing, caring, fun, and capable: ready to graduate this semester and make her mark in the social work field.

When Teri sat down in the chair and began talking, she had a look about her that I was not used to seeing—nervous, wide-eyed, and a bit apprehensive.

"Steve," she said. "I don't know what's the matter with me. This weekend all I did was go to the cafeteria and eat meals with a few friends then return to my room to write letters, read books, listen to music, and basically veg out. I'm really concerned." And on she went for the next ten minutes to describe everything she had done and thought to be a bit strange.

"Do you think there is something wrong with me? I mean I spent just about the entire weekend alone and I didn't even feel lonely!"

The smile which came over my face brought a rather puzzled look to hers. "Teri, do you see what is taking place here?" I said. "During your first couple of years at college there was no way you wanted or were able to *just* be alone. As you have become more comfortable with yourself, it has become more acceptable to be by yourself. You have done some great work on being open to your feelings and dealing them along with better understanding and meeting your needs. Congratulations, Teri!"

"Boy, am I relieved," she exclaimed. "I guess it's that I never really spent that kind of quiet time with just me, and it felt sort of good but a little scary."

Welcome to an important piece of your world, Teri. Far too few of us ever become acquainted with it. And thanks for giving us both a reality check. I can stand a little work in this area myself!

*****

If ever there was a place where the purpose is to accept people (and their problems) as they are, to encourage openness, and to facilitate healing, it is the church. For a variety of reasons as complex as the people in them, many churches and their leaders have strayed far afield from this direction.

Rather than creating an atmosphere that invites folks to discover how God and others can be a part of our struggle along life's journey, we often seem more focused on the beauty of the building, the number of programs, or the amount of the offerings.

The night before church we lay out our best clothes (our

armor?) in order to appear on top of things come Sunday morning. Then we sleep with a coat hanger in our mouth to insure a big smile when we get up. We may be preoccupied, in pain, or even arguing on the way to church, but we are able to answer *"just fine"* when asked how we are doing! With the "smile effect" (or "Smiling Christian Syndrome" as I often refer to it) beginning to fade and a sense of heaviness resurfacing, we exit the church, only to return to whatever it is that burdens us.

Sure, I know it has got to be tough being a pastor, keeping a church financially solvent, dealing with finicky boards and some odd personalities, but can't we all work on finding ways to encourage more genuineness and transparency, create emotional safety and warmth, and celebrate our differences? It's *everyone's* job to work at this—not just those paid professionals at the top.

*****

Do you remember those one or two places (literally or figuratively) you could go to as a child where it felt *safe*, where you were able to just be you, that was a harbor in the time of storm, or a sometimes secret place that seemed to know your name?

It may have been a bedroom or the basement, a pond or some woods, the stage or a ball field, a friend's house or a tree fort, intrigued by a hobby or lost in a book. Good listeners fan the flame of those familiar feelings and comfortableness with them. We feel warm, safe, and secure.

*****

Here's a special note to physicians, health care providers, prevention specialists, counselors, educators, teachers, nurses, pastors, social workers, aides, case workers, and all those associated with a helping profession: Have you invested the time and energy needed to ask yourself, "What is it that attracted me to the area of work in which I am involved?"

Those who are willing to take an honest look and inventory often gain much insight into and understanding of their own lives. They also develop a greater capacity for meaningful

167

relationships. In the long run, all of the people they are attempting to help will benefit.

It is generally no coincidence that we decide to work in the helping field. Even if it might have been a special person or positive experience that moved us in this direction, please be open to the sometimes painful issues and experiences which may also be involved. Left unacknowledged or unresolved, they will color and affect the quality and level of care we give to others.

Any good program, school or university that trains and develops helping professionals encourages and provides ongoing opportunities for their students' personal growth. The helping profession is a discipline in which knowledge of oneself can be as significant or indeed more important than content, knowledge, or the actual skills.

*****

I always apologize to the many groups that I sometimes keep late. It's really *your* fault however. You listened so well that you made me keep talking!

*****

Go ahead and keep planting seeds (listen).
Just don't forget to water (be listened to) yourself!

*****

He who trims himself to suit everyone...
(listening to everyone, every time, about everything)
...may soon whittle himself away!

*****

"I gave at the office, now I can't give at home" are all too familiar words for many of us. Never lose sight of the need to conserve energy and keep enough fuel in the tank to listen and connect with those loved ones who mean the most to us.

It's one thing to be compassionate and interested in our clients, colleagues or coworkers. It's quite another to leave at work the best you have to give.

*****

168

Living *Conscious* takes courage. Searching the depths of one's soul, the roots of our pain, and the roadways of the past is not easy going. The heart's terrain is rarely smooth and the darkness encountered is enough to send many of us packing for home.

Some of this can be done alone.

Much of it is best accomplished through the listening and direction of God and others.

Refuse the temptation to live unconscious.

Open yourself up to the *pain...* and the great *joy*.

*****

Jill was a third-year social work major and, like many of the students with whom I worked, maxed out on "busyness." She was carrying eighteen credit hours, was a member of a sorority, worked daily in the cafeteria, and was active in several campus organizations. She also had a steady boyfriend, attended a local church, and was doing a social work field placement at a nearby agency.

Jill, as with all of my students, had heard my many lectures on the "gospel of feelings," being a human "doing" vs. a human "being," and striving for balance. But I don't think it was a message she was able to relate to right then.

As class ended, Jill bounced out of her seat (more like "blasted off!"), gave a quick wave, and flew past me. I couldn't resist the urge and yelled, "Hey, Jill. Wait up! Where are you *running to?*"

Staying in stride she fired back, "I'm going to the sorority to plan for rush. Then I work at the cafeteria. Then I have a student senate meeting. Then I gotta work on a report that's due tomorrow. And then Jim and I are..."

"No, No, Jill. I mean where are you *running to?*" I asked again.

"I told you, Steve, I'm running to the sorority to..." (She angrily recited the list once more).

"No, Jill. Where are you *running to in here?*" I said as I pointed to my heart and motioned to hers.

This finally stopped her. With a rather pained and troubled

169

look, she uttered, "Uh, Oh. Can we talk about that some other time, Steve?"

We had a nice relaxed chat a few days later.

No matter if our plate is full or filled with spare time, we all have periods of running *to* or *from* something emotionally. Dealing with the underlying feelings and concerns of our life slows down the pace, promotes a sense of calm within, and curbs the urge to continually move away.

Being listened to and being heard can help us hop off the treadmill, find our center, and just enjoy being *in* our life.

*****

With his test in hand Paul knocked on my office door and asked if I had a few minutes to go over it with him. Paul usually made an "A" or "B" on my exams and his "C-" was a real surprise. His look of disappointment and frustration let me know how he felt about it. These results were out of character for him.

Five minutes into our review, I noticed the slight hint of a tear in Paul's eye and asked him if everything was alright.

"Ah, yeah, well, sure. I guess my heart just isn't into this semester. I'm not doing as well in a lot of my courses as I usually do. Wrestling has really become a drag too. I'd love to quit but I'm on a scholarship and I feel kinda stuck. It just isn't fun anymore..."

With that Paul straightened up, cleared his throat, dried his eyes, and went on to discuss the test. Once again the tears welled up and out he came with another concern on his heart.

"Things aren't so good with my girlfriend and me either. I thought we had something special and then she said it would be best to take a break from each other..." His voice trailed off.

And with that, Paul glanced at the test, composed himself, and picked up right where he left off on question #14! Amazing. This ping-pong chat we were having lasted about forty minutes. By the time we had waded through the exam, Paul revealed that he no longer wanted to be a resident assistant on his dorm floor

170

but he desperately needed the money for school. He was unsure of the major he was pursuing, and, oh yeah, "My mom and dad told me they might be getting a divorce, too."

Paul then wiped the remnants of tears from his eyes, stood up, shook my hand, thanked me, and began to leave. I inhaled deeply, for after listening to Paul's sadness, it was as if I had to catch my breath. The best I could utter was, "Gee, Paul, after hearing all that has been on your heart and mind, it's no wonder your grades are going down and you've lost interest in some things."

I felt a faint glimmer of relief in his smile, a brief acknowledgement when he began to see where some of the pain was coming from, and a slight sense of hope for possible help etched on his face. There was a tiny crack in the door, a small dent in the armor. "Let's talk again—soon," I said.

"I'll be fine," Paul responded, kicking into his "I'm a wrestler and I'll pull myself up by my bootstraps" mode.

"Paul, you're onto some pretty painful stuff here. I think it would really benefit you to keep at it," I replied.

"Okay. Sure," he said expressing little resistance. "I will."

*****

Lesson #1. What a person starts out telling you is *the problem* in his life, such as Paul's poor test grade, is often merely a smokescreen for what is really going on. The person may not even consciously be aware of the true issue. The problem could also be too painful, embarrassing, or fearful to discuss.

Lesson #2. When we begin to feel overwhelmed or preoccupied with our life's direction, there may often be several issues and emotions occurring at once. In Paul's case, it was based on five or six concerns. These issues and experiences become perceived as *islands*—separate, distinct, distant, and unattached to the others. In many situations, however, it is quite the contrary.

Many of these islands not only directly affect or entangle each other, they also consciously or unconsciously have a cumulative bearing on our energy level, outlook, and state of mind.

Get connected with your own islands.

And by listening to others, help them relate to theirs.

Lesson #3. I still have a distance to travel when it comes to tears—especially mine and other men's. Though Paul's tears were rather *frozen* and never actually released, I think they felt like a geyser to him! I had a difficult time encouraging him to express them because I am not so at home with crying in my own life. I'm getting there...

How are you with your own times of emptiness, anguish, sorrow, grieving, hurt, and tears?

What have been your experiences and feelings with another's tears and pain?

Are there certain types of issues or people with whom you are more or less comfortable in these areas?

Lesson #4. Crying is normal and natural, just like laughter. Unfortunately, the stigma remains that tears are a sign of weakness or our inability to handle things. If you don't think so, check the record of the late Ed Muskie or the other leaders who have cried in public over anything less than a horrible tragedy. Senator Muskie went from a leading presidential candidate to just another guy running for office the day after he shed some tears at an emotionally-charged session with reporters. Ask most any man or woman who is still bound by the words "Big girls and big boys don't cry."

It is most interesting that the research on crying reveals the tears elicited by peeling an onion are not the same as those shed over a painful feeling or experience. There are certain cleansing properties in our tears of hurt and sadness which move the healing process forward.

Many people cannot even remember the last time they cried.

Some see it as a badge of honor, symbol of courage, or recognition that "nothing can get to me!" We fight what should be the natural response to life's pain and gallantly fend off the tears, relegating them to a place of shame.

172

Lesson #5. If someone looks like they need or want to cry, then however you can best go about it, give them permission. A comment like...

"It's okay to cry,"

"Let 'em rip," or

"Go ahead," may work.

A simple nod of your head or glisten in your own eye may suffice. Gesturing to the box of tissues or handing over a couple of them often does the trick.

Remember, the more comfortable you become with your own tears, the more open and encouraging you will be to those of another.

You are saying without words that *"This is a safe place where hurt, tears, and sadness are welcome."*

*****

Stephen Ministry is a wonderful program which has found its way into many churches throughout America. It is a ministry of listening—not performed by the paid clergy—but by folks in the congregation. After some very intensive (and ongoing) training, Stephen ministers are paired with individuals who have a concern and need a listener. What greater ministry is there than to connect with someone on a one-to-one basis?

Incidentally, many Stephen Ministers also have to learn rule #1 of any good listener's guidebook; namely, I cannot fix another. Their motto for this is *"Caring and Not Curing."* Well said!

*****

Are you looking for a great way to sharpen your listening skills and receive the gratification of helping others? Volunteer for a telephone hot line. The training and experience you will receive is invaluable. You develop the ability to relate to others' feelings and concerns by honing in on the meaning of their words and uniqueness of their speech. With no facial expressions or non-verbal gestures to observe and read, you are left to finely tuning another facet of your perception—your *heart.*

173

*****

I've heard it said that imitation
is not the sincerest form of flattery.
Listening is!
*****

In most of the offices I have occupied, I can safely say that I
housed enough pictures, memorabilia, and stuff to start a small
museum, or at least a fun junk store. From a fish tank full of
bubbling gadgets to a puck I caught at a hockey game, from a
picture of a colorful sailboat gliding over the emerald blue sea to a
bookshelf stocked with the latest paperbacks, there was virtually
something there to catch most anyone's eye. And that was exactly
the point.

These items served as "conversation pieces." They gave the
visitor to my office something with which to identify and talk
about. It was often just enough to break the ice or serve as an
entree into a more meaningful discussion.

While it may not be necessary for you to collect or display
anything special in order to launch a conversation, what can be
helpful is for you to initially engage the speaker in a topic that is
of interest to her. Talking about something "safe" that she can
relate to builds both confidence and one's comfort level. It's like
giving the speaker something familiar to hold onto as your
dialogue moves into deeper and more unchartered territory.
*****

A task I find unpleasant and which usually gets pawned off on
my wife is making a merchandise return to a store. That and being
waited on by a harried, overworked, or unfriendly cashier are two
of my least favorite experiences. Just the expression on some sales
associates' faces make it quite clear that they are less than thrilled
to be processing my return. Clerks brace for hostile customers too!

Once you can get past taking these employees' looks or
comments personally, there are a variety of simple ways to lighten
things up and make it much more pleasant. Give one of the

174

following a try and see what happens!

- "Gee, you're not too busy today, are you?!?"
- "It looks as if you've had quite (a long) a day around here!"
- "Is the whole town out shopping today or what?!?"
- "And what time did you come in today?"
- "And what time do you finally get off today?"
  ("Not soon enough I'll bet!")
- "You must see some interesting people come and go in this place (job)!"
- "What a way (or "Tough way...) to make a living, huh?"
- "I'll bet you're glad to do another return, eh?"
- (You make one up. They're pretty easy!)

All or any part of the above lines in tandem with a smile, chuckle, sigh, or grimace can be enough to change the tenor of the ensuing interaction. I have witnessed such statements literally "disarm" a frustrated employee and turn what was likely to be a negative encounter into at least one that was palatable. A little humor and understanding can sure go a long way—whether it be with a nameless store clerk or your dearest friend.

*****

"Most of the successful people I've known are ones who do more listening than talking. If you choose your company carefully, it's worth listening to what they have to say. You don't have to blow out the fellow's light to let your own shine."

Bernard Baruch

*****

When people seem to be feeling stuck in their lives, you may want to challenge them in one of the following ways...

- "Even though you seem to feel as if you are at a kind of dead end now and are not sure what you are feeling, thinking, or need to do, try taking a guess at it."

- "While you continue to say 'I don't know' about your present situation or in regards to what decision you need to make, there is a good chance you really do have some ideas on what to do. Go ahead and take a shot at it!"

• "There doesn't seem to be a real clear or acceptable answer to this dilemma, does there? What do you think some of the solutions might be?"

• "What do you hope might happen?"

• "What would you like to see happen?"

• "What is the worst thing you could imagine happening?"

• "What are some steps you could begin taking to make some of these positive things happen?"

• "Regardless of what is going on in the lives of the people around you and possible changes they may need to make, what truth(s) do you need to recognize or accept, and what changes do you need to make in your own life?"

*****

As I stepped forward to pay the clerk, the smiling teenager operating the cash register said to me, "If I said the word "check mark" would you remember who I was?"

Caught a bit off guard, I collected my thoughts and responded with a resounding, "Yes! You are a member of the Madison High School Peer Outreach Program, aren't you?"

"You're right!" she said with enthusiasm.

People who attend my listening presentations are instructed from the outset to jot down a √ somewhere on their paper everytime they find themselves drifting off or distracted during the talk. It can be as trivial as someone walking by the door or coughing in the back of the room. Or, it might be as overwhelming as re-experiencing a hurt that gets triggered by something that is said by me or another participant.

Most check marks are brief and minor—like hearing someone sneeze, thinking of something funny, or wondering what's for lunch. Others can preoccupy us for large portions, or indeed, the entire presentation—such as how tired we are, not wanting to hear what is being said, or replaying the argument we had that morning for the fifth time.

176

My hunch is that whatever the check marks are that interfere with a person hearing me on a particular day are probably very similar to what keeps him from hearing a colleague or loved one. The more aware we become of our check mark experiences pulling us away from the speaker and her words, the better the chance we may come back to what she is saying and more effectively listen.

I asked the members in one of my workshops who attended church to try this little "experiment" in the coming week at their service. They were to keep track of their check marks during the sermon. Folks' feelings ranged from surprise to embarrassment. Some had as many as 30-40 check marks for a 20-minute sermon! They could not believe how many side trips they took while trying to focus on the sermon's message.

Can you imagine how often we become diverted during the variety of our daily interactions? Good listeners cultivate the ability to track their check mark moments, return to the conversation at hand, and focus. All it takes is a few little √√√s!

*****

Coming under the category of hearing what we want to hear:

A 91-year-old-fellow went to the doctor and had a checkup. Two days later the doctor saw his patient, smiling, with a 30-year-old woman on his arm.

"Thanks, Doc. I did what you said: 'You find a hot mamma and be cheerful.'"

"No," replied the doctor. "I said, 'You have a heart murmur and be careful.'"

From *The Executive Speechwriter Newsletter*

*****

Empathy sometimes gets confused with enabling. We can continue to maintain a measure of compassion for someone, yet not stand between or buffer him from taking responsibility for his choices or actions. Genuine love and listening often walks a fine line between caring and concern, and allowing another to be held accountable for his decisions and lifestyle.

177

*****

To "rejoice with those who rejoice, and weep with those who weep" (Romans 12:15) is often what true listening and empathy are all about. We demonstrate to others our desire to genuinely "be with" them by sharing their joy and their pain, their laughter and their tears.

*****

*Our feelings are the notes that get played out on
the musical instruments of our body, soul, spirit and life.
A listening ear can help take this rich mixture of sounds
and compose them into a symphony.*

*****

The so-called "generation gap" is actually more of a communication or listening void than a battle of the ages. I have witnessed 70-year-olds bond with 7-year-olds in unity of thought and direction. I have also seen men and women of the same age relate as if from other planets.

Willingness to listen, understand, and accept one another's feelings, ideas, and position in life is the only way we can hope to bridge that gap.

*****

What a wonderful world this would be if everyone could indeed see life from one another's point of view! Perception is a multi-faceted arena—as complex as we are complex.

One man's trash is another man's treasure.

One prisoner looks to the outside and sees freedom.

The other prisoner sees bars.

One person embraces problems as opportunities while another sees them as roadblocks.

I like Chevys. You like Fords.

Some"Jerseyites" say "wooter" and various "Midwesterners" say "warter" (even though they both think they're saying "water!")

I like the evening. You like the morning.

I say the painting is beautiful. You say "are you kidding?"

*****

Have you ever wondered why there are so many religions? And, furthermore, how can the hundreds of denominations within them all claim to have an inside track on the truth? It's all because perception is in the proverbial eye of the beholder. This in a nutshell, my friend, is perhaps *the* major reason we have such difficulty cultivating true listening abilities and accurate empathy.

I can only hear what I am *able* or *willing* to hear.

If it is out of my frame of reference, contrary to my own values and beliefs, or does not fit into my often narrow and shortsighted view of life, then forget it!

*****

Take this short quiz on perception. Read the following sentence _one time_. Count the number of "**F**s" you see (do not circle them!), turn the book over, and record the answer in your head or on a piece of paper.

> *FINISHED FILES ARE THE*
> *RESULT OF YEARS OF SCIENTIFIC*
> *STUDY COMBINED WITH THE*
> *EXPERIENCE OF MANY YEARS*

How many did you see? Most guess two, three, or four. The correct answer is somewhere between five and seven! Go back and re-read it. Did I getcha? You're in good company if I did. Not many have it right the first time.

Seeing and hearing what is actually there can be tough to do sometimes. It's a lot like really listening to another's point of view.

*****

A little girl was busily creating a collage of color with her trusty crayons. While wandering by her mom said, "Honey, that looks beautiful! What are you drawing?"

"A picture of God," she exclaimed.

"Why, no one knows what God looks like, sweetheart," her mom responded.

To which the little girl happily exclaimed, "Well they will when

179

I get done!"

Out of the mouths of babes...

*****

The comedian Jerry Seinfeld has a marvelous knack of putting a subtle spin or twist on an everyday situation that gives one a chance to view it from a little different perspective. His show is a treat to watch. My friends know not to call me when his show is on! It gives new meaning to the mundane and ordinary.

In his delightful book *SeinLanguage,* he muses, "I come from the kind of family where my mother kept an extra role of toilet paper on the tank in back of the toilet, and it had a little knit hat with a pom pom on it. I didn't know if the purpose of this was so people wouldn't know that we had an extra roll of toilet paper or because my mother felt even toilet paper is embarrassed to be what it is. The toilet paper had a hat, the dog had a sweater, and the couch arms and back had little fabric toupees to protect them. I never felt the need to try drugs growing up. My reality had already been altered."

*****

The diary of a well-known nineteenth century political figure was discovered. He wrote in one particular entry:

"Went fishing with my son today—a day wasted."

Fortunately for us, his young son (of course wanting to be like his dad) also kept a diary. Looking up the same date as his dad's entry, we found the words,

"Went fishing with my father today—the most wonderful day of my life!" Perspective, my friends. Perspective.

*****

How and where do we develop these things called perspective and perception and their first cousins, attitude and bias? They evolve from a variety of sources. Consider the following shapers and influencers...

- Friends and peers
- Community and neighborhood norms

180

- Family—including siblings and extended members
- Parents
- Teachers, coaches, and other adult leaders
- Church or religious beliefs
- TV, movies, music, advertising, and other media
- And the #1 answer!—our own _personal experience_

What have each of the above impressed upon you in regard to a particular group, situation, or topic?

How have they influenced your thoughts, feelings, and behavior in relationship to a specific issue or person?

In what ways has your perception and attitude been shaped by these forces?

We need to be open to taking an honest and objective look at the source of our biases, prejudices, and often unhealthy attitudes. If not, we risk continuing to create a kind of myopic tunnel vision—missing out on what other people and different experiences have to offer. What a shame...

*****

When our Creator made us, we were given the capacity to speak at approximately 150 words per minute (or WPMs) and a mind that could process about 1,000 words per minute!

My question to you: _"What are you doing with your spare time?"_

*****

The great Carl Jung said:

"Our neurosis is a cover for legitimate suffering."

Perhaps if more of us felt the freedom and developed the ability to be more open with our feelings, then the legitimate suffering that ultimately promotes growth would not be camouflaged by our neurotic behavior.

*****

I used to have a favorite fun assignment for my sociology students that vividly illustrated the power of perception and perspective. Three or more of them were to select the same event or

181

activity to observe or in which to participate. They had to arrive early and stay for the duration. They also had to sit in different locations from one another.

For example, if they went to a basketball game, one student could sit high up in the bleachers, another one close to the home team bench while the other might be by the visitors team bench and coach. Others might sit near the scorer's table, a group of students, a cluster of parents, or with the visiting rooters. They would have the place covered in every nook and cranny!

Following the game and with no discussion with the other students, they were to write a description and reaction paper describing what *they saw* and *experienced* that evening. At the next class they read aloud their assignments. If you didn't know better, you would never guess each had attended the *same* game! If ever a case could be made for how we see and experience things differently, this was it! It was a most *vivid* illustration.

*****

Now I never thought I was put on this earth to judge others nor have I had any formal education in this area, but I sure am good at it! If they gave degrees, I'd probably be a Ph.D. in *Judgment*! And if I had a nickel for every minute spent in judging or even giving an opinion of another, I would be a very rich man.

It seems that if a person does something contrary to what we might do, is not as good at something as we are, dresses uniquely or has different values than us, then they are somehow perceived to be less than we are. We don't always do this consciously... but we do it!

Unchecked, unexplored, and unchanged, our negative attitudes will die about one minute after we do. We carry them to our grave. Unfortunately, like excess baggage, they often suck the priceless energy and life out of so many valuable moments while we are alive.

God, help each of us to move toward a spirit of compassion and acceptance and leave the judgment behind.

Life is short enough as it is...

*****

Paul Robinson has been a trusted colleague, friend, and mentor to me. He passed on these insightful thoughts about helping that is *helpful.*

1. Recognize that some forms of help are not always helpful.
2. "Rescue" helping is occurring when:
- the helper pressures or insists that a person do/be/decide,
- the helper *has* to be helpful, or
- the helper is doing more than 50% of the work.
3. Helping is *helpful* when people:
- take more responsibility for their lives, how they feel, and what they do;
- feel more powerful, in control, and able to influence what happens to them;
- get a broader, clearer view of themselves and others and their life situation and direction;
- understand that they often cause their own problems;
- feel affirmed, prized, valued, accepted, and understood;
- can stand on their own two feet and believe in themselves and their ability to deal with life;
- are able to unload (through owning and expressing) their feelings;
- become more trusting, willing to risk, and better able to express their needs; or
- begin to change thoughts, feelings, and behaviors in ways that result in less stress and conflict in their lives that leads to greater inner peace and capacity to love.

*****

When good listeners don't agree with the speaker, they rarely do any "Yes... But(ing)"

"Yes... But" in response to another's thoughts and feelings loudly proclaims that not only do I not agree with you *BUT* I am also now going to tell you why you are wrong and I am right!

We even "Yes... But" without saying the actual words. It resides internally and seeps through in our attitude and non-verbal expressions.

Effective listeners get their point across and at the same time *affirm* that the speaker was *heard* by responding with a simple "*Yes... AND...*" statement. Big difference!

Friends, teachers, parents, bosses, and couples: *take note!!*

*****

These John Powell quotes taken from his classic book *Why Am I Afraid To Tell You Who I Am?* say so much in relation to what a caring listener can do in our lives.

"I can only know that much of myself which I have had the courage to confide in you."
"Knowing that someone loves us unconditionally enables us to face and admit our delusions."

*****

The role of listening cannot be over-emphasized when trying to better understand and assist children who live in families that hurt. The gift of our ears and support helps these kids to see more clearly the true reality of their situation rather than the distorted picture being painted by family members in deep pain.

Also, the opportunity we provide for them to learn how to hook up with a healthy adult who listens, nurtures, and clarifies will not only be of benefit today, but will also pay great dividends in future relationships.

During the week I am often home taking care of my two preschool children. If I am busy making several calls, I tend to become a bit preoccupied *and* impatient—especially if the kids are getting under foot.

It was one of those days when neither of them was responding particularly well to their dad's admonitions. I had a lot to get done and Mikey refused to cooperate as I attempted to dress him. Exasperated, I exclaimed, "Michael, would you please be still so we can get your diaper and clothes on!"

184

Observing my face and sensing my frustration, little Elizabeth came out with both an expression and words of empathy worthy of the best of social workers:

"It must be hard trying to take care of both of us, Dad."

"Yeah, uh, it can be sometimes, honey," I stammered in surprise.

Thanks for understanding, Elizabeth.

It transformed my entire day!

*****

Mike is a good friend and admired colleague. He has attempted to integrate his own personal journey of growth into the profession of being a high school principal. It is no easy task to bring stand-up honesty and compassion to a job as complex as working with students, parents, supervisors, school board members, and staff members (and they may be the toughest ones!)

Through his Gestalt Institute training he has learned to use this simple door-opening technique. When encouraging another to ponder or further process a thought, feeling, or experience he very *nonchalantly* questions:

"What's that all about?" or

"I wonder what that's all about?"

Try it. It works most every time!

*****

Mike also describes three elementary yet great questions he uses to encourage discussion with his children, students, or even friends and other loved ones. They are:

1. "What would you like to do?"

2. "Is there anything you would like to talk about?"

(and, if this gets little or no response, or the speaker is finished talking, you might pitch in with a "well there's a few things I'd like to talk about...")

3. "What do you need from me?"

*****

During the Sunday morning seminar, our facilitator and

185

pastor Dave Root was discussing how all of us have a "story." These stories are dotted (if not splattered) with ups and downs, joys and heartaches, encompassing the most ordinary to some bordering on the unbelievable.

We have one major problem as listeners.

Far too much time is often spent playing a verbal, or at least mental, game of "I can top that one," "you think that's bad," or "I thought I had it pretty rough until I heard your story. Mine's nothing compared to yours!"

This only serves to get us caught up in the speakers' factual story (details) while missing the heart of the feelings and soul of their story which resides just beneath the surface. Don't lose that!

*****

Opening up is not indicative of weakness but of *strength*.

Being genuine and telling others what is really going on is tough stuff! But doing so removes the sting from our secrets and channels the negative energy towards a positive flow.

Experiencing life head on, *conscious*, and without any chemicals, "isms," or "busyness" to medicate it, is *courageous*.

It is far easier and less risky to keep things in when we hurt than to talk about them as we hide beneath the guise of being strong.

What a paradox that in our vulnerability...

...there is actually *strength*.

*****

"Dear Ann Landers,

"I have written dozens of letters to you when I was angry, depressed, frustrated, or feeling sorry for myself. Usually I wrote late at night when I couldn't sleep.

"The next morning I edited what I had written, corrected the spelling, and ended up crossing out about 70% because I rambled too much and dwelled on things that were inconsequential. The letters then seemed hardly worth mailing because they were so short. So now I will send you what is left of the last letter I wrote. It's the only

186

one I ever mailed."

"*Dear Ann Landers,*

"*Thank you for listening. You have been a great help.*

Nelda in Appleton, Wis."

"*Dear Nelda,*

"*Your gracious letter points up one of the principle purposes of this column. Everyone needs someone who will listen. Thanks for letting me know I helped. Keep writing those letters—even if you don't mail a single one.*"

*****

Speaking of advice specialists, if you are ready for a strong dose of "reality therapy," try tuning into Dr. Laura Schlessinger's highly acclaimed radio talk show. Author of the terrific book, *Ten Stupid Things Women Do To Mess Up Their Lives,* Dr. Laura minces few words when interacting with her callers. And although you may not always agree with her style or substance, you will be compelled to consider the many nuggets of truth she dispenses about relationships, choices we make, and living more fully.

Especially helpful are her brief, yet brilliant, soliloquies sprinkled throughout the program which usually come at the close of an hour or after discussing an emotionally charged topic. Often it concerns an issue that strikes a chord in Dr. Laura's own life or is a recurring theme related to peoples' struggles.

One afternoon I dialed up her program in time to hear a most moving reflection she was giving after a particularly painful phone call. She had just spent a rather grueling fifteen minutes (that's a long time for her show!) trying in every way possible to help a caller see how emotionally abusive her boyfriend was being. Breaking into Fort Knox would have been easier than penetrating this woman's defenses. It definitely gave Dr. Laura great pause for wondering about the human condition.

After concluding the call and taking an extended commercial break, Dr. Laura returned to make a most dynamic point which sparked the following thought in me:

When you can see, feel, and hold the TRUTH in your hand (about the realities of your life, your world, your choices, and your relationships), then that is the ultimate POWER.

Indeed, our life's journey is about being *willing* and *able* to seek and accept the *Truth* about the decisions we make, people we choose to have in our lives, pain that we maintain or inflict, issues we must confront, and changes which become our imperative. Honest and challenging listeners are often the only way to discover this pathway to truth.

*****

There are lots of great self-help books available today. Entire sections in bookstores are devoted to every personal growth topic or problem known to humankind.

Reduced to merely reading them, they may take us only so far. It is often in dialoguing with another and relating the books to our own situation that these writings really come to life!

Go out and buy that paperback with the inviting title, or dust off one from your bookshelf. Read a bit and ask a friend to chat about it. Better yet, get a little discussion group together and glean from each other's rich and varied perspectives.

- What are others' thoughts and feelings on these ideas?
- What have been their life experiences in this topic area?
- How does what you've read relate to you and your situation?
- What are some of the things you might do to make any necessary changes?

Now we have a person or group of like-minded people who are moving in similar directions, who will check to see how we are doing, challenge us and give us feedback when needed, and always be ready with a listening ear.

*****

There are a host of 12 Step support groups for almost any problem, offered almost any time, and held in almost any location. Just check the local newspaper, phone book, social services, or ask around. They are there if you want to find them. The toughest step is the one that puts you through the door. After that, it's a piece of cake!

In these groups, folks gather to listen and help in any way they can. Many who attend have been close to where we have been. No one fixes. They just talk, consider alternatives, and support one another. As my friends in Al Anon like to say, "If you don't like the meeting, we will gladly refund your misery!"

Please don't try only one meeting and say "it's not for me." Go to *several*. Sooner or later you will hear *your story*.

*****

You don't have to change your basic personality to become a good listener. A little fine tuning may simply be in order.

If you have a good sense of humor, then use it to your advantage. There's nothing like a well-timed "So other than this, anything else going on in your life?" after a person just lists about five big-time concerns he is experiencing. Just remember to be sensitive and appropriate when considering injecting some levity into the discussion.

If you are the serious type, then mellow out a bit, but keep listening intently. People will appreciate how seriously you are taking them but may become put off somewhat if you are too intense. Strike a balance...

If you are the quiet one, then enjoy the beneficial silence. Keep in mind the importance of utilizing a variety of minimal prompts and non-verbal gestures. Throw in a question now and then, make a few comments, or summarize a point.

If you are Mr. Friendly, then use your gregarious nature to help others to feel more comfortable and put them at ease. Just don't over do it. Seek to blend your friendly spirit with a tone of how important you regard the speaker's thoughts.

Every person truly brings their own unique strengths to the listening equation.

*****

It is not out of line to hear a good listener respond with a "you

189

what?!?" now and then when being told about something a bit unbelievable or out of character for the speaker. Good intentioned "you what's?" or expressions of shock and amazement like well-timed humor often breaks the ice, diffuses the tension, and encourages open discussion.

*****

Most competent counselors and helping professionals will tell you that the key to successful therapy is rooted in the relationship between the therapist and the client. As significant as the professional's skills may be, equally important is his ability to establish a therapeutic relationship. Listening is usually the staircase to getting there.

As the great philosopher and baseball player Yogi Berra might explain it: 50% of counseling and helping someone is 90% listening!" Ah, sure Yogi. Well, you have the jist of it.

*****

The best talk show hosts are ones who engage their guests and audience members in meaningful dialogue. They refuse the urge to continually interrupt, cut off, or finish the speaker's sentences, nor do they give a bunch of dime store advice.

When truly flowing, they are an integral part of the show but are <u>not</u> the show itself. Good hosts exhort, encourage, empathize, and most certainly challenge. This makes for lively exchanges, helpful information, and an interesting show.

It also makes for one good listener!

*****

"For news of the heart, ask the face."
A Guinea proverb

*****

A furrowed and raised eyebrow, grimace, or wince often says
"I hear you" more effectively than the best lines or
techniques out of a counselor's handbook.

*****

We walk a very fine line between being a caregiver and a

caretaker. Caregivers work a lot of listening, challenging, and supporting into the mix while caretakers often want to advise, take care of, or just plain fix!

*****

Teachers describe an opportunity when a student seems most ready and able to learn something. They refer to it as a "teachable moment." I think the same holds true for what we might call a "listening moment." It is that time when our surroundings and a receptive spirit intersect to create a sincere desire to be open to genuinely hearing another.

These moments often come about by our own efforts. Friends, couples, co-workers, or parents and their children can do this by spending one-to-one time away from home or work—preferably in relatively "neutral" and quiet territory. A restaurant, zoo, bench, or playground in the park, while taking a leisurely walk or going on the old Sunday afternoon drive are a few possible places to discover these moments. Don't miss them!

*****

A physician friend of mine, Tom, had an interesting listening encounter one day. For several minutes he was involved in a rather intense and fruitful discussion with a patient. As the talk came to a close they both walked out to the reception area. He was quite pleased with what had just transpired between them. It's not often that a doctor and patient get the opportunity to connect on such a deep level.

Tom turned to leave and attend to his next appointment but could not help but notice his previous patient discretely whispering something to the nurse. The words she spoke brought red glows and chuckles to everyone's faces.

It seems that Tom became so engrossed in talking with his patient that he neglected one minor detail—to examine her for the reason she came to see him! Now that's focused listening!!

*****

Speaking of physicians, it is the wise and caring doctor who recognizes the many patients she sees daily whose medical problems may be linked in some way or indeed are rooted in an emotional, spiritual, or relationship concern. Her ability to listen to or refer a patient to a competent helping professional may be the true path to recovery.

*****

"The greatest compliment that was ever paid me was when one asked me what I thought, and attended to my answer."
Henry David Thoreau

*****

"Great ideas, it has been said, come into the world as gently as doves. Perhaps, then, if we listen attentively we shall hear amid the uproar of empires and nations a faint flutter of wings, the gentle stirring of life and hope."
Albert Camus

*****

Do you remember the good old days when we used to listen to something called records? They were large round plastic disks that played our favorite music. Always irritating was when one of them would become damaged and endlessly repeat the same line over and over again until someone bumped it to another groove.

(By the way, if you ever want to hear one of the funniest stories about a skipping record, just ask Larry King about his hilarious saga while a young disc jockey in Miami!)

Well, unfortunately, we encounter others who have their own "broken records" of sorts. Time and again going over the identical details or discussing the same unresolved issues, they insist we listen to their stories. Each time this happens we begin to trade our interest and compassion for increasing amounts of frustration and anger.

Would you like a suggestion or two? One would be to simply advise this person to seek someone (a professional perhaps) more knowledgeable than you are about their problem area. Another thought would be for you to hide everytime you see them coming!

And maybe the most direct, yet caring, thing you might try is to confront them with their broken record syndrome. There's a good chance that they are straining their relationships with others by doing the same thing with them.

An example of what to say might be:

"You know Joe, this is about the fifth time we have had this particular discussion. I guess I'm wondering what some things are you could begin doing to start dealing with this...?"

Or, how about trying:

"Gosh, Ellen, I can sense by how often we have discussed these things that they are really important to you. Let's see if we can't come up with some ways to begin working on them, okay?"

And, even more directly:

"Keith, I think I have lost track of how many times we have gone over these same concerns. It's getting harder for me to continue to listen to you and I feel that you need to be moving towards working these things out. I'm afraid I can't really listen anymore until you decide to take some action along those lines."

In your own style and in your own words do what you need to do in order to move people off of center and end their broken record's refrain. Your as well as their mental health deserves it!

*****

Fast food drive-through window operators and telephone order takers can teach us a lot about being a good listener. One very basic yet crucial technique the good ones use is that of calmly checking to insure that they heard our requests accurately. They simply say something to the effect of:

"Let me repeat your order back to you Ma'am. You had the...," or "Once again the price of the merchandise was $29.79 and your credit card number was Visa #5555 4444 3333 2222 with an expiration date of 10/26/98. Is that correct, sir?"

Whether they are minor details or major feelings, the best listeners always take the time to validate, confirm, and check things out with the speaker.

193

*****

In a healthy and thriving two-way listening relationship,
our conversations invariably shift from a flavor of <u>me</u> to <u>we</u>.

*****

The paradox of truly authentic listening is that:
Less is More.

*****

I had a student who took my listening workshop homework a lot more seriously than I ever would. The assignment was to contact three different people who knew them well and solicit feedback as to how they saw their strengths and weaknesses as a listener. Gary called three "exes" (wife and girlfriend types!) and asked them some rather pointed questions about how they would rate him as a listener and how he came across in his listening.

After they got over the initial shock of hearing both his voice again and his unusual request, they all said practically the same thing. In essence they told him that he was a terrific listener when he was taking care of himself physically, emotionally, and spiritually. However, when he was not doing any of those things—which unfortunately he had a tendency to do—he was a very inattentive and preoccupied listener.

Shortly after hearing his report the workshop ended. I think I'll drop him a note to see if anything has changed in his life and relationships...

*****

I have witnessed my friend and colleague Bill Ellsworth work magic in facilitating small-group discussions with his non-verbal attending skills. A nod of the head, small hand gesture, slight change in his facial expression, or the language of his eyes are enough to get the group going.

As Bill relates, among the best groups he has ever led are the ones he recalls having said only the following two words:

"Hello" and "Goodbye!"

*****

194

LETTING GO

To "let go" does not mean to stop caring,
it means I can't do it for someone else.
To "let go" is not to cut myself off,
it's the realization I can't control another.
To "let go" is not to enable
but to allow learning from natural consequences.
To "let go" is to admit powerlessness,
which means the outcome is not in my hands.
To "let go" is not to try to change or blame another,
it's to make the most of myself.
To "let go" is not to care for but to care about.
To "let go" is not to fix but to be supportive.
To "let go" is not to judge
but to allow another to be a human being.
To "let go" is not to be in the middle arranging all the outcomes
but to allow others to affect their destinies.
To "let go" is not to be protective,
it's to permit another to face reality.
To "let go" is not to deny but to accept.
To "let go" is not to nag, scold or argue
but instead to search out my own shortcomings and correct them.
To "let go" is not to adjust everything to my desires
but to take each day as it comes and cherish myself in it.
To "let go" is not to criticize and regulate anybody
but to try to become what I dream I can be.
To "let go" is not to regret the past
but to grow and live for the future.
To "let go" is to fear less and love more.

Author Unknown

While not wanting to dismiss the power of God when it comes to taking care of our struggles, diminishing our pain, or comforting us in our grief, we may sometimes unknowingly cause more hurt and anxiety by any of the following spiritual bromides:

- "Don't worry about it. God has a plan."
- "God will take care of everything."
- "It was (is) God's will."
- "God took your loved one to be with Him."
- "God is going to use this, you'll see."
- "Remember, God will never give you more than you can handle."
- "I'll pray for you."
- "Just let go and let God, okay?"

All of the above may be quite true; however, it is not always what a person needs to hear. Sometimes the greatest disservice we can do to others is to not want or allow them to have their hurt and pain.

It's fine to assure them that God is in their midst but also encourage them to simply stay with their feelings and move towards healing. As a listener, we often become like God's extension as He speaks and works through us.

*****

"For hearing all the words that slipped away...
...for knowing all the feelings I didn't say."
American Greetings card

*****

Have you ever seen yourself on videotape or heard your voice on a tape recorder? Pretty scary, eh? Usually the first words out of your mouth are, "that's not really me. You doctored up the tape!

Few of us see ourselves as we really are. That's where trusted and valued listeners help to fill in the missing pieces of our life's puzzle. From a gentle nudge to a forceful shove, they encourage us to become acquainted with our unfamiliar parts—those we have been unwilling or unable to see and experience.

196

*****

"Don't talk unless you can improve the silence."

Author Unknown

*****

What Kind of Listener am I as Seen Through the Eyes of Another?

(This little assignment has been a real eye opener and favorite of many of my students. I even had one brave soul contact some ex-girlfriends. Did he ever get an ear full! I have also had a number of folks get some invaluable insights. Do it on a *regular* basis!)

Sit down with (or even write, phone, e-mail, or fax!) three or more people in your life who know you well, interact with on a regular basis, and from whom you are *willing* to receive some open and honest feedback. Consider a spouse, good friend, parent, child, family member, neighbor, co-worker, colleague, boss, student, "ex-something," or whoever.

Interview each one using the following questions. Feel free to throw in a few of your own. Don't forget to really *listen*. There could be some very enlightening lessons involved.

1. Overall, how do you see me as a *listener*? *Rank* me on a scale from #1-10 and *explain*... (#1 = Lousy! #10 = Great!)

2. What are some *specific* things I do which indicate that I am *not listening* to you (verbal and non-verbal)?

3. What are some *specific* things I do which make you *genuinely feel heard* by me (verbal and non-verbal)?

Good luck!

*****

Flash to the middle of the night and Snoopy is nervously scurrying to be with his buddy Charlie Brown. Charlie says...

"Are you upset, little friend? Have you been lying awake worrying? Well, don't worry... I'm here. I'm here to give you reassurance... Everything is all right. The flood waters will recede... The famine will end... The sun will shine tomorrow...

And I will always be here to take care of you! Be reassured!

Cut to Snoopy fast asleep, with a contented smile, on top of his doghouse. Now travel to Charlie Brown's darkened bedroom. Wide-eyed with covers pulled up to his chin he feebly questions:

"Who reassures the reassurer?"

Who are the *"reassuring listeners"* in your life?

*****

Abe Lincoln, arguably one of our greatest presidents, was faced with a most monumental decision—one with the possibility of pitting family against family, with literally brother fighting brother. Abe contacted a longtime and trusted friend from Illinois and requested that he come to Washington immediately.

Dropping everything and traveling day and night he made it to the White House. Upon being warmly greeted by the president, he was asked to be seated and Abe began talking.

Late into the evening President Lincoln shared his fears, weighed his thoughts, and examined every possibility. As the discussion waned, his friend having virtually said nothing, Abe thanked him and sent him on his way.

Can you imagine traveling that distance under such rugged conditions, finally arriving at your destination, engaging in a lengthy one-sided conversation, and then being asked by your friend to turn around in the same evening and go home?

Well, as they say, the rest is history. The next day Abe Lincoln took the steps necessary to plunge our nation into a war that would change it's very foundation. The President, like you and me, needed to be heard, sort a few things out, and most importantly, to *hear himself*. Using his friend's ears, eyes, and heart as a sounding board, Abe knew what he needed to do.

*****

"Know what I like about our relationship?

"I like the way I can call you when I have absolutely nothing to say and neither do you and there is just dead air over the phone line but somehow, it's just nice to feel connected and it doesn't matter much that we have nothing to talk about because I know that if I did have something to say, You'd listen...

"...There aren't many people I can 'not' talk to like that."

American Greetings card

*****

"Dear Readers:

"Mark Twain was a silent participant at a dinner party in Hartford, Conn., one evening. When he was chided afterward for not saying anything, he replied that his host had talked so incessantly as to leave little opportunity for any conversation.

"It reminds me of the man who was reproached by a friend, who said, 'I think it's a shame that you have not spoken to your wife for 15 years. How do you justify it?' The husband replied, 'I didn't want to interrupt her.'"

Taken from a recent "Dear Abby" column

*****

"And in the naked light

I saw 10,000 people, maybe more

People talking without speaking

People hearing without listening

People writing songs that voices never share

No one dared, disturb the sound of silence"

By Simon and Garfunkel—excerpted from the "Sound of Silence"

*****

Funny that as we get on in years and become more "mature," we tend to minimize those feelings and experiences of people which seem less painful or important than our own. We especially do this with those who are younger than us.

Consider a couple of examples:

#1 "You're upset because your girlfriend dumped you? It happens all the time. That's nothing compared to all that I've been through! First I get a divorce I don't want, and then I lose my job.

#2 "Mommy, Mommy, that boy down the street broke my favorite truck," little three-year-old Johnny exclaimed. "I hate him, Mommy!'

199

"You shouldn't hate him, Johnny. Besides, it's no big deal. You have plenty of other toys to play with," his mom responded.

"But I loved that truck, Mom, and now it's gone," Johnny said.

"That's enough, Johnny," his mom fires back. "If that's the worst thing that ever happens to you then you're a lucky boy. It was only a cheap little truck. You can just get another one."

Ah, yes, it was only a toy truck. Not an expensive adult toy like her car and her home, or the other *big* things in her life that were all messed up. "That's nothing compared to what I am going through right now," was among many of the thoughts spinning around in his mother's mind as she listened to Johnny's plight.

By the way, Mom also missed a great opportunity here to connect with her son and provide a learning opportunity about feelings. He really didn't "hate" the boy for breaking his truck. What do three-year-olds know about hate anyway? He was hurt, angry, and sad. All perfectly normal feelings to have and appropriate ways to respond in such a situation. Interpret the word "hate," Mom, and allow your son the freedom to feel.

When distilled to their basics, isn't much of our pain and many of our difficult experiences all *relative*. Even though the fellow's breaking up with his girlfriend may not seem like such a big deal, it is to him. It appears less significant when compared to the man going through a divorce and losing his job. And although Johnny's broken truck looks less important than his mom's personal problems—it still hurts a lot.

No matter what the age, no matter what the circumstances, and no matter what the situation—what may not be deemed essential (and indeed may even seem rather trite) to us—might very well be extremely meaningful to another. Respect that...

*****

Have you ever heard different people describe the same accident they witnessed or an event they each attended? If you didn't know better, you'd swear that none of them were in the same place—all thanks to those little invisible filters tucked away in their heads and their hearts. They can sure create some fascinating scenarios and paint amazing pictures!

Ask an insurance claims adjuster, law enforcement officer, or news reporter about eyewitness descriptions they hear on a daily basis. They could tell you one unbelievable story after another.

- "He was a very tall man." "No, he was a rather short fellow."
- "The lady was wearing a bright red dress." "No, she had on black pants. I'm sure of it."
- "The car pulled out this street over here." "No, the car turned down that street over there."
- "It was early evening." "No, it took place around lunch time."
- "I saw at least 300 people." "No, at the most, there couldn't have been more than fifty in attendance."

Here are a few of my personal favorites of accident reports taken from actual insurance claim forms...

- "The guy was all over the road. I had to swerve a number of times before I hit him."
- "I pulled away from the side of the road, glanced at my mother-in-law, and headed over the embankment."
- "I was on my way to the doctor's office with rear end trouble when my universal joint gave way causing me to have an accident."
- "As I approached the intersection, a stop sign suddenly appeared in a place where no stop sign had ever appeared before. I was unable to stop in time to avoid the accident."
- "An invisible car came out of nowhere, struck my vehicle and vanished."

Once again, the power of perception personified.

*****

"Do you have a minute to talk, Steve?" Sandy inquired as she stopped by my office one afternoon. (By the way, be wary of the person who only needs a "minute" of your time. It's often closer to a half an hour!)

"Sure Sandy. Have a seat," I said.

201

Sandy was a senior social work student. Knowing her as well as I did, I didn't figure it was anything too serious, nor something we couldn't handle. She began to chat about her college softball team. Being a big fan of baseball and softball, I was prepared to enjoy and engage in the conversation. What I was not ready for was the sharp curve ball about to be thrown my way.

Sandy loved playing softball and was looking forward to a fun final season of her college career. Unfortunately, the coach had other plans and decided to "rebuild" the team by playing underclassmen. This left Sandy rather dejected and spending a lot of time on the bench.

I did not hear much of what Sandy said over the next twenty minutes. You see, I, like Sandy, once lived for playing the game of baseball. I too had a conflict with my college coach, ended up cut from the team, and found myself cast into a spiral of hurt, anger, and depression.

Even though I was more than ten years removed from this experience and felt as if I had worked it through—surprise!—I really had not put it to rest. As Sandy got up to leave, I realized that emotionally I had been an absentee listener. I asked Sandy to come by in a day or two to talk some more. I knew that once I had a moment to collect my thoughts and sort out a few of these feelings, I would be able to hear her much better...

*****

What do you do when a person begins to tell their story and before long something in it strikes a familiar chord? If you are like most of us, you have to fight the sometimes overwhelming urge to interrupt him and start in with your own experience. If, unfortunately, you are like some of us, you simply succumb to the temptation and begin talking right over his words!

There is certainly justification for wanting to tell him that you can relate to his story, for many times our experiences can be of help. And, if nothing else, it might be rather comforting to know that another person has gone through something similar.

Initially though, what he needs most is for us to tuck away our own feelings and memories and try to focus on his. This is one of the toughest things for listeners to do. But if we don't, we miss the subtle details as well as the significant pieces to his story.

Here are some good ways to diffuse the preoccupation with our own story, encourage him to continue exploring and sharing his, and at the same time make him aware that we too have been there—so to speak. A simple, "You know, Jack, I went through something real similar to what you are going through. I know how it affected me. How's it been for you?"

Or, you might try, "Gee whiz, Jack, does what you are telling me ever sound familiar! I sure can relate to a lot of it. I'm wondering how you have been handling things?"

Another one could be, "Hey, Jack, I've been down that road before! I know a little bit about it. Here's how it made me feel (or, "here's what it did to me..."). I'd be interested to hear a few of your thoughts and feelings about it."

These are easy yet sure-fire techniques which help stoke the conversational fires, keep the door open, and prevent us from "one upsmanship" or diminishing another's story.

*****

We have feelings for a woman or a man which are similar to the ones we have for our mother or father. A person has certain physical characteristics or even looks and sounds a lot like someone else in our life. We encounter people who have a sense of humor, kind of philosophy, or way of thinking that distinctly reminds us of a friend or acquaintance. A certain name or title may be enough to elicit a particular emotional response.

Although not the classic psychological definition of transference, for our purposes that is what we shall call it here. Frequently we are around people who for any number of reasons remind us in some way of another person we know. It happens all the time.

We go away to live and during the first few months it's as if everyone we come in contact with looks, talks, walks, laughs, or acts like someone back home. We are often not very conscious of what is taking place. We then may experience a somewhat positive or negative feeling towards this person which in turn dictates how we will interact with her.

This has significant implications for our ability or willingness to listen to others. If the transference is along positive lines, we can hear the person much better. If the transference takes a negative bent, then we may be quick to tune her out.

Whenever you have a fairly strong reaction to a person (ranging from "I don't like him" to "From the moment I met him, I really liked him!")—especially upon your first meeting or just getting to know him—you might want to ask yourself:

"Is there (or has there ever been) a person in my life she reminds me of?" "What is it about her that causes me to feel a connection?" Or, "Why is it that every time I am with her she really seems to push my buttons?" You just might find a little transference going on. Check out the following example...

As I walked into the men's department, I could hear the salesman brusquely talking to the customers. While flipping through a rack of suits, he came over and politely said to me, "May I help you, young man?"

Startled, I stammered, "Why, uh, yes, you can. I just got a new job and need to find some dress clothes."

"That's great," he responded. "Let's see what might work."

For the next twenty minutes he gave me his undivided attention. The only time he left my side was to curtly answer a customer's question or to quickly ring up a sale. He even kicked a teenager out of the dressing room to make a space for me! After trying on the items, I asked him if he would put a few of them aside while I shopped around. "Sure, son," he said. "I'd be glad to."

After looking elsewhere, I decided I liked the suits I saw in the first store best. I called the salesman and asked him to hold them until the next day.

"No problem, young man. I'll have them waiting for you," he said. As I was hanging up the phone I could hear him grumbling at yet another customer.

The next morning I went to get fitted and pay for my suits. His resonant voice could be heard booming throughout the store. When he saw me coming, he walked away from a customer and grabbed my suits. He carefully measured me and marked the clothes. Whatever did I do to deserve such treatment—especially in light of how he treated his other customers?

While writing my check, he opened up his wallet and pulled out a picture. "You know, Steve, I have a son about your age. He lives in another state and I don't get to see him much. I really miss him. You remind me a lot of him," he said.

Well this explains everything, I thought. This is why he was so warm and friendly to me and seemingly so indifferent, even downright rude, to so many others.

This transference thing is powerful stuff!

By the way, there was some transference going on with me also. It's pretty funny too. You'll never guess who he reminded me of? He not only looked (short, stocky, and a crew cut), but sounded (loud, bellowing voice) and acted (gruff exterior, warm-hearted interior) a lot like Sergeant Carter from the old Gomer Pyle show. Can you picture this guy now?

*****

Our world, so advanced in technology and ways to communicate, is still full of individuals hungry to connect more intimately with others. What do you think some of this obsession with the Internet is all about?

As a substitute for genuine human contact—in which people can look one another in the eye, catch the tone in their voice, and sense the true message of their hearts—we are relegated to a kind of pseudo relationship with a faceless partner. It's safer and less risky than the real thing. There's a lot less chance that we will get hurt or too involved.

205

All we need to get started is a discount computer, inexpensive modem, subscription to an online service, and the time we would normally spend with our families, friends, or in developing new or deeper relationships. Perhaps we have reached the age that the best selling book "Megatrends" predicted—one best described as "High Tech" and "Low Touch."

Internet fans do not take this the wrong way! There are some terrific benefits to going online. Some view it as a kind of return to the days of letter writing. Just be wary of allowing it to devour your time and energy or become a substitute for personal contact.

*****

One of the most helpful things we can do to become calm within and open to another would be to develop the art of prayer, meditation, and a few relaxation techniques. Try taking a yoga class, attending a wellness workshop, and attempting to be more prayerful throughout the day. You will be amazed at how becoming more "centered" can make you a more *mindful* listener.

A little breathing technique may be a good place to begin. To the count of 3-4, simply breathe in slowly and deeply through your nose. With pursed lips, exhale in similar fashion.

If you can do two things at once, repeat some positive brief words as you inhale ("I am calm," "I am relaxed," or maybe a short saying or verse you like of an encouraging or spiritual nature). As you exhale, breathe out your stress and tension. Do this regularly and not just when you are feeling anxious or stressed.

Becoming aware of your breathing helps you to become more aware of yourself. And this can make for one *dynamite* listener!

*****

I assumed this book was finally completed until I heard these most profound words from Rev. Jim Smith of the First Presbyterian Church, Shelby, Ohio. While participating in a recent "Listening Connection" workshop, he thoughtfully observed:

"Good teachers may not necessarily be good listeners,
but good listeners always make good teachers."

Jim went on to relate this compelling aspect of listening:
*"Out of the chaos of peoples' words, thoughts, and feelings
often comes a new reality. These insights bring about fresh
perspectives which become a kind of 're-creation' in their lives."*

*****

As I put the finishing touches on this book, our country is
reeling from two tragic airline disasters—the Valujet crash in the
Florida Everglades and TWA's Flight 800 from New York to Paris.
The nation feels a collective heartache as we watch the friends
and family members grasping for answers that may never come
and mourning their loved ones. The sadness seems unbearable.

We see caring volunteers, clergy, and other trained
professionals surround those who are hurting and attempt to
bring whatever comfort they can. Almost to a person, when
interviewed by the media, they all say basically the same thing:

"There is nothing we can humanly do or say that will take
away or lessen their pain. It's a pretty helpless feeling. What we
are able to do though is be with them and *listen*. More than
anything, that's what they need now to move towards healing."

Thank God for these courageous and selfless listeners. They
are true angels of mercy.

*****

In a variety of ways and by a number of people I have heard
the following words:
*"When we are open and ready to learn something about our life,
our purpose, our struggles, and our relationships...
...a teacher will come into our life."*

Many times these "teachers" will take the form of wonderful
listeners. The lessons we need to learn are shaped by the magic of
their receptive spirit and in listening to our inner voice.

I trust that you discovered something in this little book that
drew you nearer to your own life's lessons and gave you pause to
reflect upon how you might experience what it means to become
that teacher and listener for another...

207

Voices In The Fire

Daddy!

Daddy!!

DADDY!!!

The pleas were familiar ones.

Maybe he was thirsty. His tank always seemed to be on empty.

Perhaps it was a bad dream. We were talking monsters outside his bedroom before he went to sleep.

Or could we be paying the price for that late night drink I gave him? I'm a sucker for that, what can I say?

I prayed it would not be the thing I dreaded most—that infrequent occasion when this energetic four-and-one-half-year-old arises in the middle of the night, up for the duration, and exclaims, "Let's play baseball, Dad!"

These were about the only thoughts I could muster at this time of night. With one eye on the clock and the other eye begging it to be joined in rest, I began to inch my way out of bed. What day is it? Did I miss my alarm? Oh, no! I'm late for work! Haven't you ever shot straight up in bed, wide-eyed and in a state of panic, convinced you had overslept—only to realize it was the weekend? Ah, a reprieve. The clock read 4:22 a.m. and, better yet, it was Saturday.

But as I fumbled to find the bedroom door and slowly tugged at its handle, I was not prepared to meet the stranger that awaited me on the other side. Continuing to hear the cries of "Daddy, Daddy, my throat is dry," a loud alarm was blaring in the background below while billows of choking smoke met me at the stairway.

"The house is on fire, Sue. We have a fire!" I screamed.

I took three steps down the stairs to see what I could do and realized the next step would be my last. My knees buckled. The smoke was suffocating. I all but passed out on my feet.

Sue was now beginning to stir. She could sleep through a

208

train wreck. I think she thought I was on some new early morning aerobic fitness program where I ran up and down the steps yelling, "Fire! Fire!"

When Sue realized what was happening, she kicked right into our fire escape plan which, most miraculously, we had just discussed a few short days before.

("Hey Sue, what do you think we should do if we ever have a fire?" I asked.

"Well, Steve, I think we could call for help from the upstairs phone and then squeeze through the bedroom window onto the kitchen roof," she said.

"Us. Through that?" I said, pointing to a window that measured eighteen inches by fourteen inches. Maybe we could have wriggled through when we were young—in our fantasies about thin bodies or for a dire emergency. But we'll never have to worry about that, I thought.)

As I grabbed Jeremy, Sue rammed open the window and gently shoved us out. She then yanked the comforter off the bed and followed us with phone in hand. What a picture—the three of us huddled together on the roof—scared, confused, and freezing in the chilly February air. Sue called the fire department and then some good friends.

Just what do you say to a friend in this situation? "Hey, we're having a fire and are on the roof of our house. Do you want to come over?"

The next few moments were some of the longest in my life. There's just something about sitting on your roof at 4:30 a.m. on a brisk February morning that has a way of altering one's perspective. Why can't we human beings take a fresh look at things or make a change in our lives without having to have a "fire experience" motivate us?

As I peered around the corner of the roof, I could see the bright orange, blue, and yellow flames jumping up in the dining room window. It looked like the same beautiful fire that had cooked the hot dogs for our winter picnic that evening in the fireplace of our new home which ironically we had just finished painting, decorating, and remodeling. In fact, this morning we were to do the last of the touch-up painting.

It was like watching a person rob and vandalize your home at gunpoint while you could do nothing about it. What helpless and unnerving feelings washed over us.

In the distance, we could hear the sirens. It seemed to take forever. This only happens to other people, doesn't it? Geez, I hope they're coming to our house! Please God, I hope the cats are okay.

Sam, Liz, and Lil—what a threesome. Sam was my in-law's feline. We were cat sitting. Liz and Lil were like Sue's kids, and I must admit, after not caring a whole lot about them early on, they had become special to me too. I just wish cats didn't have cat hair! And to think only a few short hours ago we were chasing Sam all over the neighborhood after she had escaped from the house. We both had the claw marks to prove it. Maybe she had a premonition of what was to come.

"They're here! Do they know we're on the roof. Hey, over here!"

One by one they very calmly got us off the roof and into the emergency van. My son had the excitement of going down the ladder with a real fireman. The fireman had the thrill of carrying my wife down in her nightgown (Did it really take five of them to do the job?).

"Hey, I'm up here too you know!" Then I went.

"How are you guys doing? Do you need any oxygen?" one of the firemen asked. Jeremy was a brave little guy and Sue was her usual level-headed strong self. I don't know what I was.

"Hey, here comes Sam."

Dazed and in shock, she began to perk up when they gave her some oxygen.

"It's Lil. They got her too!"

Lil was in sad shape. Having had her unconscious body stepped on and drenched by the water, she was smoky and limp.

210

They used an infant's oxygen mask on her and she began to revive.

"We had the black and white one in our arms but she leaped away. We don't know if she ran in or out of the house," said one of the firemen.

Later that morning little Liz was found curled up under a neighbor's back yard barbecue grill. The three girls are doing fine and even my fish made it. We re-named him "Firebeater."

That night I woke up at 3 a.m. seeing imaginary smoke and frantically searching all corners of the house for a non-existent fire. We watched in horror as the next evening's top news story reported on an Akron couple who had called the fire department from their bedroom window, just like us. They never made it out.

Our vivid memories and Jeremy's bad dreams have subsided but I still get a knot in my stomach when I smell the burning leaves of a neighbor or hear a fire truck roaring down a street.

Well, it has been quite a while since that very eventful, and yes, perspective-changing day in the life of our family. Many tears have been shed, hugs given, words of support offered, and the monumental task of rebuilding has been completed. Seventy-seven days and $47,000 later, we were back in our home. It was a heckuva way to redecorate.

Quite amazingly, our wedding pictures and family portrait— located right on the fire's travel path—were untouched. The camera which took the pictures of our evening's fireplace picnic and weiner roast was a melted mess—but somehow the film survived and the photos returned unscathed and perfect. A brief note and disclaimer from the photo lab accompanied the photos. It read, "film may have been heat damaged." No kidding!

We are thankful for skilled and caring firemen and construction workers, and a sore-armed claims adjuster who wrote countless checks with huge numbers that I was not used to seeing. They would have made the best of social workers proud with their ears of compassion and words of encouragement.

211

The love and care of friends and family sustained us throughout, and the weeks spent living at my in-laws confirmed one thing: they are the greatest. Rose Ann's wonderful cooking netted me ten new pounds. And what more can be said about a father-in-law who gobbles up sporting events on the tube with a passion equaled only by his son-in-law, yet often gave him first dibs on the remote control flicker? When Ralph, an affectionate Archie Bunker, said, "Pass the rolls, Meathead," I knew I was in.

Thoughts come at the least expected times, usually while riding in the car somewhere or completing a mindless task.

The words of the firemen and construction crew are etched in my memory.

"You know, just about two more minutes and the fire heading up the dining room walls to your bedroom or the smoke charging into your bedroom would have gotten you. Your bed would have fallen through the floor into the fire, or the smoke would have silently killed you. You were real fortunate."

And, indeed, we were. For my son's screams are what initially woke me up, not the smoke detectors. They were going off as they sat in a closet waiting to be hung that day on our freshly painted walls. I couldn't hear them until I got out of our bedroom.

When Brian and Brenda, two of Sue's longtime friends, heard about the fire, they called us immediately. They are two of the most spiritual (and I don't necessarily mean religious) people I know. God is a personal part of their everyday life. After asking if there was anything they could do to help, Brenda said, "We prayed for you every day." It seems that the week preceding the fire they had felt a special sense to keep us in their prayers.

"Thanks, Brenda, we appreciate that. We'll let you know what you can do, okay?" Sue said.

As Sue was about to hang up, Brenda continued...

"Sure, Sue. But there's one other thing you need to know. Brian woke up today at _4:20_ a.m. out of a deep sleep and felt compelled to pray for all three of you."

At 4:22 a.m. Jeremy's cries got me out of bed.

Some "coincidence," huh?

Life is indeed about listening—to *God*, to *others*, and to *ourselves*. The "old" Steve would have kept going down the steps to try and fight the fire. The "new," improved model listened to his heart and his head when they said, "go back upstairs and take care of your family. What's more important—saving your family's lives or trying to be a man and fix everything?"

Are you getting better at listening to that inner voice?

Thank goodness I listened to Sue when as I headed back into the house she grabbed me and exclaimed, "Where do you think you're going? We're staying right here on the roof and waiting for the firemen!"

Are you more willing to listen to and consider the insights, challenges, and feedback of another?

How amazing it was that our dear friends were so attuned to God's voice. Most people would have ignored those words and gone back to sleep!

Are you open to the possibility that your Creator is speaking to you everyday—if only you would take the time, become quiet within...

...and Listen.

ENOUGH

of the constant stream of self help books,
parade of new-age gurus showing us the way,
plethora of ivory tower motivational speakers,
endless magazine articles on fixing our life,
volumes of "how to" videos, and
insufferable infomercials.
Just go out and
LISTEN

NOW!

It is well worth the effort, my friend...

When There Are...

No words for the unspeakable,

No feelings for the untouchable,

No thoughts for the unthinkable—

May God bring a Listener into our

life, or guide us to be that Listener

for another, so we might connect

with and return home to

Ourselves.

Steve Powers, October 27, 1995

To purchase additional copies of
"LISTEN TO YOUR NEIGHBOR'S HEART"
please send a check or money order for $14.95 +
$3.00 for shipping & handling to the address below.

To inquire about our other services and products contact:

The LISTENING CONNECTION

356 North Townview Circle • Mansfield, Ohio • 44907
Internet E-Mail Address: Wehearyou@aol.com
Call Toll Free: 1 - 888 - 252 - 0229
Phone: 419 - 756 - 9117
Fax: Same #

Here are a few of the workshops and special presentations
Steve Powers provides for a variety of groups and organizations.

♥ The Listening Connection ♥ The Power Of Personal
Wellness ♥ The Language Of Feelings ♥ Kids, Drugs,
Alcohol, And You! ♥ Listen To Your Neighbor's Heart ♥
15 Pathways To Personal Wellness ♥ Building Healthier
Relationships ♥ Saying Goodbye Doesn't Mean Forever
♥ Living In Today: The Art Of Being Present ♥ Intimacy
Is More Than A Three Letter Word! ♥ Working With
Kids And Families That Hurt ♥ Necessary Changes:
Their Pain And Their Power ♥ Perception And
Paradoxes: It's All In How We See And Experience It! ♥
Basic And Advanced Support Group Facilitator Skill
Building ♥ Fit, Fat, Or Fed Up: The Profound Effects Of
Diet And Fitness ♥ Stress Management Revisited: A
Fresh Look At A Tired Topic ♥ Student Assistance 101
♥ Takin' It To The Streets: Peer Helping, Prevention, And
Outreach ♥ The Chemical Dependency Dilemma ♥
Leadership Programs ♥ Team Building ♥ Employee
Assistance And Wellness Programs ♥ You Name It And
We'll Try Our Best To Design And Provide It For You!!! ♥